Amazing North Carolina

★ ★ ★

Fascinating Facts, Entertaining Tales, Bizarre Happenings, and Historical Oddities from the Tarheel State

T. Jensen Lacey

Rutledge Hill Press™
Nashville, Tennessee

A Division of Thomas Nelson, Inc.
www.ThomasNelson.com

To every Tarheel—by birth or by heart

Published by Rutledge Hill Press, a division of Thomas Nelson, Inc., P.O. Box 141000, Nashville, Tennessee 37214.

Library of Congress Cataloging-in-Publication Data

Lacey, T. Jensen (Theresa Jensen), 1955–
    Amazing North Carolina : fascinating facts, entertaining tales, bizarre happenings, and historical oddities from the Tarheel State / T. Jensen Lacey.
        p. cm.
    Includes bibliographical references and index.
    ISBN 1-55853-965-4 (pbk.)
    1. North Carolina—Miscellanea. 2. North Carolina—History—Miscellanea.
I. Title.
F254.6 .L33 2003
975.6—dc21   2002153074

Printed in the United States of America

03 04 05 06 07 — 5 4 3 2 1

CONTENTS

FOREWORD

From the magnificent Blue Ridge mountains to the pristine beaches of the east, North Carolina is full of beauty in its land and in its people. The Tarheel State boasts some of history's most fascinating and determined individuals and was the birthplace of some of mankind's greatest achievements. It was this determination that first powered flight on the shores of Kitty Hawk.

In *Amazing North Carolina*, T. Jensen Lacey captures stories and facts that help paint a colorful picture of life in the Old North State.

—Governor Mike Easley

PREFACE

After writing my latest in what I call my "Amazing America" series, I have to admit I've fallen in love with yet another state. That place is called North Carolina. From her breathtaking mountains to her crystalline shores and all places in between, the Tarheel State is full of wonders. In researching for this book, I discovered fascinating stories and incredible tales, and also had the great fortune of meeting some of the friendliest people on earth.

Whether they were famous, infamous, or just regular folks, the people of North Carolina that I met caused me to realize that they are what make the state great. If you live within its borders, you're lucky. If you haven't visited yet, you're missing out on a state that makes the United States a wonderful place.

Even if you are a long-time resident of North Carolina, you are sure to read some tale within these pages that will reveal a fascinating tidbit you didn't know. Read on and discover why North Carolina is a state of endless mystery, beauty, and charm.

ACKNOWLEDGMENTS

No project is ever completed by one single individual, and the same goes for *Amazing North Carolina*. Here are just some of the "amazing" people I would like to thank for their contributions, patience with my questions, photographs, or expertise, or for just putting me in touch with the right person. Besides the hundred or so people who were helpful in myriad ways, special thanks go to the following: Governor Mike Easley for writing the foreword; Greer Beaty and Bill Teague of the North Carolina Department of Commerce for all their help; James and Martha Pearl Villas, cookbook authors and North Carolina personalities, for their "bereavement" recipes; Kathleen Mosher and Barbara O'Neil for the Biltmore House story; Linda Ball and Randy Schumacher with the North Carolina Film Commission in Raleigh; Laura Chase with the Asheville Convention and Visitors Bureau; Albemarle's Christine Dwyer for the many interesting tidbits and photos she shared; Jaime Amoroso, botanist with the North Carolina Natural Heritage Program, for information on the Venus flytrap; Lance Holland of Fontana Village and Fontana Dam for help and hospitality; Lloyd Childers for information on the history of the Corolla wild horses; Patrick Glynn of Wireless Flash News Service for researching more than fifteen years' worth of amazing stories related to the Tarheel State; John and Diane Fitzgerald for their hospitality and recipe for the corn they let me try (unforgettable, both); Steve Anderson and Cheryl Oakes of the Forest History Society in Durham for the photos and stories relating to the lumber industry and history of forestry in the state; John Joyner at the Charles B. Aycock Historic Site for the story on the "education governor"; Tom Melton in Bostic for his story on Abe Lincoln's Tarheel roots; Bob Huggett and Horatio Beck for some great coastal stories; Sallie Anderson in Yanceyville for the stories on the hanging cell, the unsolved murder of "Chicken" Stephens, and the accidental invention of bright-leaf tobacco; Tarheel author Ralph Grizzle for his encouragement; Erica Derr, administrator of *Our State North Carolina* magazine, for the myriad ways she helped in my research; Captain Skippy Winners and Doug Medlin for their stories of the blockade runners and the sunken vessels off the coast, and Cathy Medlin for her hospitality; author Thomas Fairley and Jean Beasley for information on sea-turtle rescues; historian Max Williams of Cullowhee for his railroad expertise and checking the convict burial-site tale; Dawn Frazier of the Topsail Island Chamber of Commerce for her help and hospitality; Kim Rupard, group tour coordinator of Grandfather Mountain, Inc., for information and photos of Mildred the Bear's cubs; Dave Moore and Connie Mason of the *Queen Anne's Revenge* Project and of the North Carolina Maritime Museum for their help with related stories, and the tale of the Chanteymen; Jackie Bolden of the Folkmoot Festival for her help and photos; in Raleigh, Parker Call for the walking tour and LeRae Umfleet for the Cherry Bounce story; Steven Case, Jason Tomberlin, Debbi Blake, Melissa McGee, Ron Vestal, Jo Ann Wiliford, Alice Cotten, and especially Stephen Massengill of the North Carolina State Archives and History office for information, assistance, photos, and for not calling me a pest when I was; Officer Frank Etheridge for the tour and stories of the North Carolina Supreme Court Justices; sports writer Jim Sumner for his help on the sports chapter, and for looking it over for me; James Moore, Esq., for reading and checking the final version of the entire text from the point of view of a fourteenth-generation Tarheel; Jacksonville historian Kim Kimball for his stories; Shannon Leissner of Pittsboro for the story on the Carnivore Preservation Trust; Shelagh Donaldson of Salisbury for an exceptional job of providing all kinds of stories and tidbits; Greensboro's McArthur Davis for the story of the Woolworth's sit-ins and the update; Karen Reynolds, playwright and historian, for reading the story about Tom (Dooley) Dula; Paul Becker and David

Olson at Riverside Cemetery in Asheville for digging up many great cemetery stories for me; Smithfield's Billie Stevens for her expertise on and photo of Ava Gardner; Marilyn Howarth for those great seafood recipes and for the story and photo of her grandmother, the legend behind "Mrs. Calabash"; Doug and Donna Bennett at the Aerie in New Bern and Al and Catherine Blalock of Cameron House in Raleigh for their recipes, stories, and hospitality; Brian Burgess of the Eastern Band of the Cherokee Nation, *a-ho* (Cherokee for thank you) for information on stories relating to the Principal People; and Wolf Furstenau and Paul Becker for Civil War tales.

To Candler friends Mark and Vicky Taylor, thanks for putting me up— and for putting up with me, during my research. To all my friends both in and out of the Tarheel State, thanks for listening to my stories and giving me feedback. Thank also to Larry Stone, president of Rutledge Hill Press, for choosing me to write yet another book under the RHP imprint, and to Jennifer Greenstein, my editor, and the entire staff of RHP and its parent company, Thomas Nelson.

Finally, thanks to my daughter, Sarah, for taking so many of the photographs I used in this book, and for being navigator extraordinaire during my excursions. To Eric and my son, Gus, thanks for waiting patiently while I went on sometimes wild-goose chases and interviewed people all over the Tarheel State. To my parents, and mom- and dad-in-law, your expertise, help, and support were invaluable, as usual.

And last of all, to those who read this book, I thank you. If you can think of anything to add to the next edition, please contact me in care of my wonderful publisher.

1
Truly Bizarre Events and Notorious Criminals

These Brothers Were Really Close!

Born in 1811 to a poor couple in Bangkok, Thailand (then Siam), twin brothers Chang and Eng shared everything. When one got sick, so usually did the other. When one laid down for a nap, his brother followed. When one went for a walk, his brother joined him. The brothers had no choice: Chang and Eng were the original Siamese twins, joined at the chest.

When they were fourteen years old and working as peddlers on the streets of Bangkok, they met a Scottish trader named Robert Hunter, who introduced them to American ship captain Abel Coffin. Coffin saw the marketable possibilities in the pair right away, and smelled money.

Coffin brought Chang and Eng first to Boston, where they were a hit; from there, he exhibited them in New York, then London, where they were invited to tea with the Royal College of Surgeons. For a time, they were part of Phineas T. Barnum's circus.

When they were twenty-one, Chang and Eng parted ways with Coffin and Barnum and decided to tour America on their own, exhibiting themselves for fifty cents. First they became U.S. citizens, and took the last name Bunker from a Fred Bunker they met by chance in the New York naturalization office. In 1837 Chang and Eng Bunker's two-man show took them to Wilkesboro.

The twins fell in love with the beauty of the mountains and decided to make their home there. They also met and fell in love with Sarah and Adelaide Yates, the daughters of a Wilkes County farmer. Although it seems the father initially opposed the marriage, finally the four married in the local Baptist Church. Chang married Adelaide, nineteen; Eng married Sarah, who was one year older. The twins' twenty-second birthday was the next month.

They built their homes one mile apart near Mount Airy. When they weren't touring, the brothers had a visitation pattern from which they never varied: they spent three days at Sarah's house, then three days at Adelaide's. The first child—a beautiful boy—was born to Adelaide and Chang. Eng fathered twelve children, and Chang ten.

When Chang and Eng Bunker's two-man show took them to Wilkesboro, they fell in love with the scenery and decided to make their home in the area. (Courtesy N.C. Office of Archives and History)

The twins were not alike in their personalities. Chang enjoyed his drinking, while Eng abhorred the stuff. Chang liked to stay up late, while Eng was more of what we call a "morning person."

Chang's health began to deteriorate after a stroke, after which he began to drink even more heavily, despite his brother's pleas to stop. Finally, in January 1874, Chang's health took a turn for the worse. He came down with bronchitis and although physicians told him to stay in bed, it was time for the brothers to go to Eng and Sarah's home. Eng was reluctant to move Chang (and thereby himself), but Chang insisted.

During the night, Chang's

breathing became labored and then his heart stopped beating. When Eng awoke and found his brother dead, he also passed away—some say of fright.

You can see their tombstone where the brothers are buried in the old White Plains Baptist Church, two miles west of Mount Airy, on old U.S. 601. They were joined later by their wives, Sarah and Adelaide.

This Is a Real "Hair-loom"

In Fayetteville, Dick Lambert's wife made her own wedding dress. But this wasn't your everyday wedding dress, with lace and satin—this one was made with human hair. His wife spent nearly a year making the all-white dress, weaving in curly, straight, and braided locks. When she died in 1994, Lambert put the dress up for sale, to the tune of $50,000, but so far, no takers.

The Unsolved Murder of Beautiful Nell Cropsey

In 2001 Elizabeth City marked the hundredth anniversary of the mysterious death of one of its own southern belles, Nell Cropsey. The story continues to intrigue and confound even the most persistent sleuths—and the home from which she disappeared is reported to be haunted by her spirit.

Elizabeth City is a lovely town in the northeast part of the state, on the banks of Pasquotank River near the Albemarle Sound. Ella Maud Cropsey, known as Nell, was one of the more celebrated beauties of the town, with light brown hair and piercing blue eyes.

She attracted many admirers, and by the time she was eighteen all expected her to make a brilliant marriage and settle down as one of the town's matrons. But this was not to be. Nell had a steady admirer, Jim Wilcox, but as time went on with no marriage proposal, the couple began to have disagreements.

On the night of November 20, 1901, a young man named Roy Crawford called on Nell's sister, Ollie, at the same time Jim called on Nell. Jim and Nell were the first to go to the front porch to say their goodbyes, and when Ollie and Roy came outside to do the same and saw neither of them, Ollie assumed Jim had left and Nell had slipped upstairs to the bedroom the two girls shared. But when Ollie went to their room, Nell wasn't there.

Legend has it that Nell's father, William Cropsey, sat in the back of the house near the kitchen eating prunes, and so was unaware of these goings-on. When Ollie awoke some time later and reported her sister still absent, neighbors and family set out to search for her. Thirty-seven days later, Nell's body was found in nearly perfect condition floating in the Pasquotank River.

She was carried home and an autopsy conducted in the summer kitchen revealed that Nell had been killed by head trauma. Then the speculations began.

Jim Wilcox said that he and Nell had had a falling-out the last night she was seen alive—as a matter of fact, he said he had broken off the relationship, leaving the young beauty weeping forlornly on the front porch.

The young man denied having seen Nell since he left her on the porch. The father said he saw and heard nothing that night. Wilcox was jailed under suspicion of murder, and guarded by reserves called out by the governor.

A lynch mob came to the jail, but was dispersed by Nell's father. Wilcox was tried for the murder in 1902 and sentenced to hang. A mistrial was declared because of public disturbances during the trial; at retrial Wilcox was again convicted and sentenced to thirty years in prison. The Cropsey family left the area, and Nell's sister Ollie went into seclusion.

Tragedy after tragedy hounded the people surrounding Nell and her disappearance. In 1908 Ollie's old beau Roy Crawford shot himself to death. In 1913 Nell's younger brother, Will, took poison and died in Norfolk, Virginia. In 1918 Governor T. Walter Bickett pardoned Wilcox, and although Wilcox and W. O. Saunders (the editor of the Elizabeth City newspaper, the *Independent*) planned to collaborate on a book about the mysterious disappearance and death of Nell, Wilcox kept backing out. In 1934, also for reasons unknown, he committed suicide.

There is still much speculation about the nationally infamous unsolved murder, but Robin Caruso, the current owner of the house, believes the father killed his daughter accidentally.

"The night Nell disappeared and shortly after the suitor had left, her father heard their pigs squealing in the backyard," Caruso says. "Seeing a figure running in the yard, and thinking it was a pig thief, he shot at the person, striking the head. Then, I believe, Nell's father and sister realized it was Nell the father had shot. They brought the stricken girl back in the house, to try to secretly nurse her back to life and health. When they failed and she died, they put her in the river so no one would suspect the father. That explains the nearly perfect condition of the body. In other words, although she had been missing for thirty-seven days, she had only just recently died when her body was discovered in the river."

Today, the house seems to be haunted by the spirit of one whose murder will never be solved. The son of the owner, near in age to Nell at the time of her death, says he has seen her, and others have heard noises and seen objects move in the house.

If you go to Elizabeth City, be sure to see the beautiful homes, walk by the piers and shoreline of Pasquotank River, and enjoy the friendliness of the people and the great seafood. You cannot tour the home of Nell Cropsey, but you can drive down Riverside Avenue and see it for yourself. Maybe you'll see her face in a window, perhaps waiting for the suitor who will never come back or for her own murder to be solved, once and for all.

"Just Hanging Around" in Caswell County

In the town of Yanceyville you can tour the Old Jail, which has a curious history.

Built in 1906, the Old Jail contains the only remaining hanging cell in the state. When docents open the great iron door to the cell, you can see a hangman's noose and a trapdoor beneath it. That trapdoor is controlled by an iron handle next to the stairs that mount to the floor where the inmates lived. There you'll get chills as you view the bare springs of the iron bunkbeds, the ancient plumbing fixtures, and the stark metal walls displaying graffiti left by prisoners of long ago.

The ironic part is that the hanging cell was never used, as the last public hanging in Caswell County was in 1902 and hanging cells were outlawed while the Old Jail was still under construction. The last ne'er-do-wells inhabited the Old Jail in 1977.

Besides being entertaining, the hanging cell may offer another, more pragmatic value. Parents can show their unruly children the Old Jail, and the sight of the hanging cell with its trapdoor can work wonders on the kids' attitudes.

The "Devil's Tramping Ground"

Ten miles from Siler City in western Chatham County off North Carolina 902 is a strange, uninhabited spot surrounded by trees. It's almost a perfect circle, about forty-four feet in diameter, and barren of vegetation. Siler City residents say that even the birds won't make nests in the trees near the strange circle. It's been like this for more than two hundred years, long enough to become a place of legend. Locals know this privately owned land as the Devil's Tramping Ground.

Some say that nothing grows in this area because Old Beelzebub paces here, night after night, as he plans his mischief for the souls he desires. Others say the place remains bare because it is a sacred place: Native American people are said to have celebrated victories in war or hunting here.

A related story holds that two warring Native American tribes battled here and Chief Croatoan, the leader of one of the tribes, was killed in the fray. The legend says that he was buried in this circle before his people fled to the coast. There they met with the surviving members of the Lost Colony, and agreed to join forces with them, explaining why the word "Croatoan" was carved on that famous tree in Roanoke (see "The Enduring Mystery and Legacy of Roanoke," in Chapter 7).

A more scientific explanation is that the high salt content of the area has rendered the soil sterile, and a number of soil samples have borne this out. This doesn't explain, however, why sticks placed within the circle are found moved the next day or why hunters' hounds on nighttime forays refuse to go near the area.

Whatever the reason, the circle remains bare, and the cause of this bizarre barrenness remains open to speculation.

The Mysterious Origins of Judaculla Rock

In the town of Cullowhee is a sandstone boulder covered with pictures and prehistoric messages. They have never been deciphered, and although the Cherokee discovered it on their land, the pictographs have never been attributed to any specific tribe or time in history.

Legend says that the pictographs are actually the footprints of a giant. The Cherokee call him "Tsul'kula," and say that he lived in a mountaintop home here.

You can go see the footprints—or pictographs—for yourself. The mysteriously marked outcropping now known as Judaculla Rock is six miles past the town of Cullowhee, near the intersection of U.S. 441 and Caney Fork Road.

Now You Can Feel Safe from Aliens

Those who worry about the possibility of alien abduction can rest easier. Robert Null of Maiden has invented a UFO detector. The detector senses changes in magnetic activity, which Null says allows aliens to defy gravity.

Robert Null of Maiden invented a UFO detector that responds to changes in force fields.

UFO detection, like medicine, is not an exact science. "We don't exactly know what UFOs are," Null says, "but some of the reports filed by policemen and military people indicate there's a force field emitted by aliens because strange things happen when they are near, such as cars starting on their own and things like that. From this, it appears UFOs have some kind of gravity control and maybe an electromagnetic force associated with them."

Null builds a variety of small electronic devices that respond to changes in the earth's magnetic field, extraneous magnetic forces, and gravity. "This is just a concoction of devices that can sense force fields," he adds. Null says he keeps at least one of his devices on him at all times, and although "a UFO event is rare in North Carolina," one never knows—and he wants to be prepared.

"I haven't seen UFOs myself," he admits, "but I have seen changes in my instruments due to magnetic storms and changes caused by the sun and some things associated with earthquakes."

Null has been selling his devices since he invented them in 1996. "It takes about a week to build one of these things," he says. The cost ranges from fifteen to thirty-five dollars.

Bath and the Mysterious Hoofprints

About a mile outside the small town of Bath in Beaufort County is one of the greatest unsolved mysteries of North Carolina. If you drive along the Goose Creek State Park Road just off U.S. 264 and wander about two hundred and fifty yards into the forest, you'll find a trail. Near this trail is a series of round, shallow depressions, ranging in size from large saucers to plates. Nothing grows in these strange, barren shapes, which have been here for more than a hundred and fifty years. If the depressions are filled or if things are placed or planted in the holes, the next day they are just as empty and barren as before. A number of possible explanations exist for this strange phenomenon.

The most popular legend holds that one gentleman of Bath was so obsessed with horse racing that he defiantly did so on a Sabbath, saying to his horse as he took off, "Take me in a winner or take me to hell!" The reckless man, Jesse Elliott, was killed instantly when his horse threw him against a tree. Some locals say the marks are the horse's hoofprints, made by a horse delivering a "man on his way to hell." The depressions are, indeed, in the pattern that a running horse might make.

Whatever the reason for their existence, the mysterious hoofprints of Bath remain, along with the legend handed down by each generation.

Pardoning a Legend

On May 1, 1868, a young man named Tom Dula was hung in Statesville for murder.

To tell the story, we have to go back to just before the Civil War. Young Tom and a girl named Anne Foster were childhood sweethearts. Dula had a reputation for being lively at social gatherings, playing the fiddle, and flirting with the girls. Tall and good-looking, with dark curly hair, he must have stolen many a heart before he became a soldier in the Civil War.

The war separated him from Anne. While scores of women waited for their husbands and beaus to return, Dula returned to find Anne married to a man named James Melton. Then Dula began courting Anne's cousin, Laura Foster.

As time went on, although he and Laura were regarded as a couple, Dula couldn't deny the love he and Anne still felt for each other. He began visiting another cousin of Anne's, Pauline Foster, who was their accomplice in helping Anne and Tom see each other. The plot thickened when Laura realized she was expecting Tom's child.

In May 1866 neighbors saw Laura riding her father's horse toward the ridge (now called Laura's Ridge) where she and Tom often met—and it was the last anyone saw her alive. When the riderless horse returned home, Laura's father and others began searching for her.

Laura's body was found, stabbed to death. Hearing the news and realizing he was the prime suspect, Dula fled to Trade, Tennessee, where he stayed with a man named Colonel James W. M. Grayson under the assumed name of Hall. Meanwhile, Pauline blurted out her role in the affair. Anne was also implicated.

Officials found Tom through Grayson; the young man was then extradited to Wilkes and tried for Laura's murder. He was convicted and again found guilty after his appeal resulted in another trial.

At age twenty-two, Tom was sentenced to hang in Statesville. The night before his hanging, he scrawled in pencil a single sentence to save Anne from sharing his fate: "I declare that I am the only person that had any hand in the murder of Laura Foster." Next morning, as he stood by the gallows, Dula declared his innocence in the murder. Legend says his famous last words were, "I am only guilty of loving two women."

The sentence was carried out in front of three thousand witnesses on May 1, 1868. Tom's sister, Anna, brought the body to the family homestead in Elkville (now Ferguson), and buried him in a coffin made by her husband. Tom rests near a bend in the Yadkin River close to the intersection of North Carolina 1134 and 268 West, near the Caldwell County line. A historical marker is near the spot where he is laid in his final resting place. And, in case you were wondering, Tom's sweetheart, Anne Foster, lived to a ripe old age. But that's not the end of the story.

The headstones of Laura Foster, who was murdered in 1865, and Tom Dooley, who was hanged for the crime in 1868. (COURTESY DR. DAVID SPICELAND, APPALACHIAN STATE UNIVERSITY)

In North Wilkesboro, a playwright named Karen Wheeling Reynolds began writing about the legend of Tom Dula. As she continued her research, Reynolds became intrigued about the trial and the lack of evidence against Tom, and the fact that Dula professed his innocence even up to the moment of his hanging. The playwright spoke with other townspeople about her increasing conviction that Dula was innocent. When she was finished, the play she wrote, *Tom Dooley: A Wilkes County Legend,* had picked up so much interest and momentum in the community that it sold out twelve performances before it opened in July 2001. ("Dooley" is the local pronunciation of the name "Dula.")

Locals began to think it was time to reconsider the case and have Dula pardoned. Ken Welborn, publisher of the local newspaper, the *Record,* went so far as to secure the services of a local law firm to start the paper trail. McElwee Law Firm wrote a petition asking for Dula's posthumous pardon from Governor Mike Easley.

The town's mayor, Conley Call, issued a proclamation in July 2001 asking people to sign the petition, which was forwarded to the governor's office in Raleigh. Wilkesboro residents held a month-long celebration of their history and heritage in July 2002, calling it "Dooley Days." This event, which includes the performance of the play, is now an annual occurrence.

Reynolds believes Laura's murder will remain a mystery. "I believe people are not comfortable with what happened, and that's why even after all this time, there is still this interest in getting him pardoned," she says. "I don't think he'd write a confession one night, then tell a lie at the gallows. And Pauline wasn't a credible witness, and didn't have to back up what she told the authorities."

The tragic story of Tom Dula was retold in quite a few songs. One, recorded by the Kingston Trio in 1958, includes the lyrics "hang down your head, Tom Dooley," and caused a surge of interest in folk music. If Dula is pardoned, then maybe the Kingston Trio will sing a slightly different song about Tom.

N★C Stran@e . . . but true

During the Civil War, Tom Dula befriended Joseph Blevins, who later went by the name Isaac Watson. Blevins/Watson became a journalist for the *New York Herald*—and one of his first assignments was to cover the trial and subsequent hanging of his friend.

Before Viagra, There Was "Goat Gland" Brinkley

John Romulus Brinkley was a native of Jackson County, born near the end of the 1800s. Always believing he was destined for greatness, he set his sights on making a name for himself in the world of medicine and undertook the study of the healing arts—by mail. In 1911 he was granted the title of "undergraduate doctor" by the North Carolina Board of Medical Examiners, and went on to earn his medical degree by mail from the Eclectic Medical University of Kansas City.

Most medical boards were loath to grant Brinkley a medical license with such a dubiously earned degree, but Brinkley finally found that Arkansas would honor a medical diploma from Eclectic. Once Arkansas granted him a license, other states followed suit, and he gathered licenses to practice medicine in Texas, Connecticut, and Kansas. By 1917 Brinkley was practicing medicine in Milford, Kansas.

Still searching for a way to make his name a household word, Brinkley began reading about how ancient peoples revered the goat as the most sexually potent of all animals, and also of old legends in which goat-like men mated with human women.

He announced to the world that he had discovered a way to transplant goat testicles to men, thereby increasing men's virility and potency. After a childless man from Wakefield impregnated his wife following the procedure, Brinkley's bizarre operation became his own pot of gold.

Patients lined up for the surgical procedure, each paying the required

$200, and Brinkley was obliged to build a fifty-bed hospital on borrowed funds. The price of goat testicles rose to $1,500 a pair; still more patients filled the hospital beds, awaiting their own miracles. Shortly after 1921, however, the American Medical Association stepped in and charged Brinkley with fraud and "gross immorality." They took away his Arkansas license, but Brinkley quickly moved to Mexico, where he established a radio station, WXER. He used the station to garner even more fans (and funds), answering medical questions on the air for a small fee. Those "small fees" poured in, making Brinkley even wealthier. By the time the inevitable lawsuits occurred, Brinkley had amassed a fortune of more than $10 million.

Before the U.S. courts in San Antonio could take action against Brinkley for medical fraud, he ran for the U.S. Senate. Although Brinkley's name has all but disappeared from historical annals, this story has one more strange twist. In this particular Senate race, Brinkley was beaten by a man whose name later became synonymous with Texas history: Lyndon B. Johnson.

One "Hairy" Tale

In Macclesfield, the townspeople came up with a way to celebrate their centennial on May 12, 2001. The men spent all of March and April growing their beards, with prizes for the Best Beard, Worst Beard, and Most Creative Beard. Revenues were generated by fines to men who either shaved before May 12, or who refused to grow facial hair at all.

The contest drew the attention of Aramis in New York, a division of Estée Lauder, which

Edwin Webb, a participant in Macclesfield's centennial celebration, was the first to shave off his beard in the old town jail, using a can of donated Aramis Shave Cream. (COURTESY ARAMIS/KAREN TAM)

decided to sponsor Macclesfield's "hair-raising" venture. They dubbed the event "Shave-A-City," and used the competition to promote one of their oldest shaving products. "It's called Aramis A+ Shave Cream, and people love it," said Jennifer Witt, an Aramis publicist. "When we heard about the city's beard-growing venture, we decided to get involved with it, and turn a 'Town with Hair' into a 'Town That's Bare.'"

Only in America . . .

The Haunting of the Double-wides

You can hear many stories about beautiful mansions haunted because they were built over Native American burial grounds, or because someone died under tragic circumstances there before the new and naive owners bought it. But what about the poltergeists of the trailer parks?

Comedian and musician Larry Weaver of Chapel Hill claims that, yes, ghosts do indeed haunt mobile homes and trailer parks. Weaver's album, *Looking for Fun,* features the song "Ghost in the Trailer" about a family terrorized by a "redneck ghost." His website, www.trailerghost.com, includes warning signs to look for, such as moving eyes in the velvet Elvis painting or the trailer shaking with no tornado in sight. At the workplace, if Nehi strawberry soda comes out of the coffee machine, you can assume your trailer ghost has accompanied you to work! If you think you may be haunted by a redneck ghost, don't worry—Weaver offers trailer-ghost-busting kits via his website.

"Bald Is Beautiful" in Morehead City

Television celebrity Willard Scott and former President Gerald Ford are in it. So were the late Yul Brynner and Telly Savalas. "It" is the Bald-Headed Men of America Club, of which John T. Capps is head . . . er, president. Capps lost most of his hair before he was thirty, and while it didn't bother him, he knew that hair loss did bother some people.

Capps decided to create a club promoting pride in bare pates, and moved from his home in Dunn to Morehead City to establish the club's headquarters. (His reason for the move lies in his favorite expression, "*More head,* less hair.")

That was in 1974. Now the club has grown to include more than ten thousand members from all over the world. Capps promotes his club with gag gifts such as toothless combs and hosts a "Bald Is Beautiful" Convention in Morehead City every second weekend in September. During the festivities, club members vie for titles such as Most Kissable Bald Head or Sexiest Bald Head. The contest uses celebrity judges (in years past Erma Bombeck was one).

Think they split hairs over a tie?

John T. Capps gets kisses on his pate from three attendees at the "Bald Is Beautiful" Convention in Morehead City. (COURTESY JIMMY SPARKMAN, PHILADELPHIA, PA.)

When Blackbeard Terrorized the Coast

The most feared and notorious pirate ever to be seen off North Carolina's shoreline was the Bristol-born, bloodthirsty Blackbeard (his given name may have been Edward Teach or Edward Drummond). He and his crew stole a French merchant's ship, outfitted it for piracy (complete with forty cannons), and renamed it the *Queen Anne's Revenge*. This became his flagship and the beginning of his diabolical fleet. The sight of Blackbeard's ship and his countenance alone put many a captain and crew of a mind to give way, and with good reason.

Accounts agree that Blackbeard was a big man, with black hair and a long black beard. Blackbeard was perhaps one of the first to use psychological warfare in battle, and intimidation was a big part of his success. Before boarding another ship, he would light slow-burning artillery fuses, which he had braided into his beard. The sight of the tall, swarthy figure mounting their gunwales, his beard and grim countenance surrounded with smoke and sparks, filled many a crew member with dread. Often ships were surrendered without even a skirmish.

He was a ferocious fighter, once going up against a thirty-nine-gun British man o' war—a daring, reckless act, which few other pirates would attempt. By the early 1700s, Blackbeard and his fierce crew had acquired a squadron of vessels and continued to torment the merchants plying the waters of the Atlantic between Europe and the Carolinas. Blackbeard's favorite haunt was the area around Ocracoke Island, on the Outer Banks. It was within striking distance of the rich port of Charleston, which allowed Blackbeard to continue his friendship with Charles Eden, the governor of North Carolina. Eden pardoned Blackbeard for extortion, after which the pirate wedded a sixteen-year-old girl (some say this was his eleventh wife, others say she was number thirteen) and temporarily settled down in the coastal town of Bath.

In Virginia, Governor Alexander Spotswood was angered at Blackbeard's coddling and decided to offer British sailors the chance to wreak revenge on the "Terror of the Black Flag." In November 1718 Spotswood sent Lieutenant Robert Maynard and a squadron of ships to sail to Ocracoke to attack the pirate. Blackbeard and his crew tried to flee, then fought. For many crew members, including the infamous pirate, it was a fight to the death. (Note: Blackbeard's famous ship, *Queen Anne's Revenge*, has been discovered and is being salvaged. You can read about in "Lost and Found: The *Queen Anne's Revenge*," Chapter 10.)

Blackbeard received twenty-five wounds that day and literally lost his head. When Maynard sailed back to Virginia, he had the pirate's head on the bowsprit. Although piracy continued along the Atlantic seaboard, the death of the most infamous pirate of all time was the beginning of the end of piracy.

Did You Know? Blackbeard's house—what's left of it—is accessible, but only by water. It's located where Bath Creek and Cack Creek meet, at the end of Main Street in the town. Rumors persist that the pirate buried gold around there, but nothing has been found so far.

The Mysterious Murder of a "Scalawag"

In the town of Yanceyville on May 21, 1870, John Walter "Chicken" Stephens was murdered in the backroom of the Caswell County Courthouse. Referred to by his peers as "a notorious scalawag," this politically manipulative and inflammatory man was hated by such a great number of Caswell County residents that the identity of the assailant was a mystery. At the time of the murder, many people were milling around at the courthouse, so more than two hundred people were held in the county jail that summer as suspects for the crime. (This may be the record for the greatest number of suspects ever held in jail for a single murder.) According to Yanceyville historian Sallie Anderson, although no one was ever definitely named as the killer, the murder was believed to have been the work of members of the Ku Klux Klan.

Today, you can take a tour of the courthouse and see the room where the murder occurred. You can also see Chicken Stephens's pistol, taken from him at the time of the murder, on display at the Richmond-Miles Historical Museum, also in Yanceyville.

N★C TRULY BIZARRE TRIVIA

Q. What world record is held by Hendersonville twins Billy and Benny McCrary?

A. They are the world's largest twins, each weighing eight hundred pounds.

Q. What curiosity in the Belhaven Memorial Museum must be viewed with a magnifying glass?

A. The "flea wedding," complete with a tiny church and dried-up fleas dressed in full wedding regalia.

Q. What town has a "ghost light," said to be the spirit of lantern-wielding Joe Baldwin, a train engineer who was beheaded in an accident in 1867?

A. Maco. The light is called Maco Railroad Light or simply Maco Light.

Q. What stuffed animal can you find in the Fireman's Museum in New Bern?

A. Fred the fire horse. When he died on the job (pulling a hose-wagon) in 1925, the firefighters decided to have him stuffed. Fred is now on display in the museum.

Q. Where was the world's first university-based parapsychology laboratory established?

A. At Duke University in 1927, by Dr. Joseph B. Rhine, who is now regarded as the "Father of Parapsychology."

Q. What small building in Salvo holds (nearly) a national record?

A. The post office. At 8 x 12 feet, it's the second smallest in America, beat only by the Ochopee, Florida post office, measuring 7 x 8 feet.

Q. What was the name of the "emergency hospital" hurriedly constructed in 1945 in Catawba County in response to a polio epidemic?

A. The "Miracle of Hickory."

2 Politics

Abraham Lincoln: Tarheel By Birth?

Some people in Rutherford County insist that "Honest Abe" was *not* born in Kentucky, but took his first breath in Bostic. Here's the story—honest!

In Rutherford County around the latter part of the eighteenth century, a woman named Lucy Hanks made her living by spinning for local families, and she bore two daughters, Mandy and Nancy. Unable to provide for them herself, Lucy Hanks put her daughters in the care of local families. Nancy was placed with a farmer-teacher named Abraham Enloe and his wife.

Not long after the turn of the century, Enloe and his family moved to a farm near the banks of the Oconaluftee River. At the time, unbeknownst to everyone, Nancy was in the family way. When the situation became apparent, Abraham Enloe's wife was understandably upset.

Nancy disappeared for a few months and when she returned, she brought along her newborn baby boy. Enloe made an offer to an itinerant laborer, Tom Lincoln: take a team of horses with all the accoutrements, some money, Nancy and her son; marry her and move to Kentucky.

Apparently this was an offer Tom couldn't refuse. The result? Although the history books claim that Abe Lincoln was born near Hodgenville,

Tom Melton stands beside the historical marker in Bostic that states "Honest Abe" was born not in Kentucky, but in Rutherford County, North Carolina. (COURTESY MIKE MELTON)

Kentucky, Rutherford Countians say Abe was born on *their* soil and that he was named after his birth father, Abraham Enloe.

People who lived in Rutherford County around 1809 (when Abraham Lincoln was born) swore that Nancy had returned to the old Enloe home place to give birth, and that they had seen her and her baby there. The story was further borne out by J. C. Coggins, a Rutherford County–based legislator and teacher, who in 1920 wrote a book entitled *Abraham Lincoln: A North Carolinian with Proof.*

Tom Melton, a resident of Bostic in Rutherford County, believes he has found the remains of the old Enloe place and the site of Honest Abe's birth. For the price of lugging a stone to the site (to further mark the historic place), this former principal and teacher will lead you down a two-mile path through the woods along the banks of Puzzle Creek. There you can see the remains of an old stone cellar, all that is left of what locals claim to be Lincoln's true birthplace.

If you don't have the time for a hike in the woods, you can more easily see the plaque commemorating what is said to be Lincoln's true birthplace. In 2000 the Historical Society of Rutherford County erected a granite plaque at the intersection of Walker Mill Road and Bostic "Sunshine" Highway (N.C. 106). The plaque reads:

Traditional Birthplace of Abraham Lincoln
The Sixteenth President of the United States
One Mile East

Why the Name "Tarheel"?

Various reasons explain why the people of the Old North State are nick-named "Tarheels." Here are the two most persistent.

The principal products during the state's early days—turpentine, pitch, and tar—came from the great numbers of pine trees within its borders. As processors worked with these substances, they got them on the soles of their shoes.

The second story, however, is much more entertaining. Legend holds that during the Civil War the fiercest fighters hailed from North Carolina. In one battle, Union forces drove back the forces supporting the North Carolina troops, but the North Carolina soldiers stood their ground. When General Robert E. Lee heard of what had happened, and that the North Carolina soldiers had held fast as though they had "tar on their heels," Lee is said to have commented, "God bless the tarheel boys."

North Carolinians have proudly called themselves by that moniker ever since.

Did You Know? Among the original thirteen colonies, North Carolina was the first to vote for independence from England. North Carolina became the first colony to declare its complete independence from Britain in 1776 in the document entitled the Halifax Resolves, drawn up after the Battle of Moores Creek Bridge.

The Greensboro Sit-ins

On February 1, 1960, four black college students made history when they entered the downtown Woolworth store in Greensboro and purchased school supplies. Then the four—Ezell Blair Jr., Franklin McCain, Joseph McNeil, and David Richmond—calmly took seats at the "Whites Only" lunch counter. The young men, all Tarheel natives, sat there the whole day, waiting to be served. They probably didn't realize their actions that day would be the flashpoint behind the national civil rights movement.

The sit-in was a denouncement of segregation, a nonviolent plea for African American people to receive the same treatment as white people. Although the young men didn't get served that first day, they determined to return every day to the lunch counter.

The Greensboro lunch counter sit-in occurred every day for six days, with each successive day seeing a growing number of college students crowding the lunch counter, until Woolworth was forced to temporarily close its doors. The students then suspended their "sit-ins" to allow the merchants in the community time to desegregate their shops and restaurants.

It was a painful and tumultuous time, and some people paid for their beliefs through violence and even death. The Greensboro lunch counter sit-

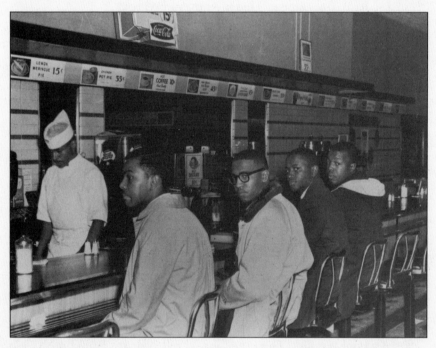

When college students Ezell Blair Jr., Franklin McCain, Joseph McNeil, and David Richmond sat down at the Woolworth lunch counter in Greensboro, they probably never imagined the impact their actions would have on the national civil rights movement.
(© GREENSBORO NEWS AND RECORD. USED WITH PERMISSION.)

ins, some of the first civil rights demonstrations in the United States, made history and caused America to reflect on injustices, eventually creating new laws to replace archaic ones.

Today, Greensboro is a thriving and cosmopolitan town that embraces diversity while remembering its past. You can see exhibits about the Woolworth sit-ins at the Greensboro Historical Museum. In addition, an International Civil Rights Center and Museum is now located in the old Woolworth building, and you can discover even more about local diversity at the Mattye Reed African Heritage Center.

Official State Symbols

Here are some of the state symbols of North Carolina, and the year the General Assembly made them official:

State Symbol	Year
Flower: Dogwood	1941
Bird: Cardinal (or Winter Redbird)	1943
Toast: "The Old North State"	1957
Tree: Pine	1963
Shell: Scotch Bonnet (bo-NAY)	1965
Mammal: Gray Squirrel	1969
Fish: Channel Bass	1971
Precious Stone: Emerald	1973
Insect: Honey Bee	1973
Reptile: Turtle	1979
Rock: Granite	1979
Historic Boat: Shad Boat	1987
Beverage: Milk	1987
Dog: Plott Hound	1989
Vegetable: Sweet Potato	1995
Fruit: Scuppernong Grape	2001
Berries: Strawberry and Blueberry	2001

During the presidency of James K. Polk, Sarah Polk is said to have initiated the playing of "Hail to the Chief" every time the president entered the room. (LIBRARY OF CONGRESS)

Hail to the (Vertically Challenged) Chief!

The tune "Hail to the Chief" was first played at the inauguration ceremony of Martin Van Buren in 1837. Sarah Childress Polk, however, is said to be the person responsible for the tune being played every time the president enters a room. She started this during the presidency of her husband, Pineville-born James K. Polk, who took office in 1844.

President Polk was five feet, six inches, not particularly tall for a man. As a result, his entry often went unnoticed, and this annoyed Sarah. She had the White House band play "Hail to the Chief" so everyone in the room would take note of her husband's entry.

Every president since then (vertically challenged or not) has continued with this musical tradition.

Here are the words, so now you can sing along.

Hail to the Chief

Hail to the Chief we have chosen for the nation,
Hail to the Chief! We salute him, one and all.
Hail to the Chief, as we pledge cooperation
In proud fulfillment of a great, noble call.
Yours is the aim to make this country grander,
This you will do, that's our strong, firm belief.
Hail to the one we selected as commander,
Hail to the President! Hail to the Chief!

—Words by Albert Gamse; music by James Sanders

Guess Who? In 1824 four men ran for president of the United States: William Crawford of Georgia, John Quincy Adams of Massachusetts, Henry Clay of Kentucky, and a North Carolinian. The Tarheel candidate won the most popular and electoral votes, but lacked the majority of electoral votes mandated by the Constitution. So the decision went to the House of Representatives, who chose Adams. When Adams appointed Clay as the new secretary of state, our Tarheel candidate suspected that the two had struck a deal to "rig" the election. Four years of bitter accusations of corruption followed, but in 1828 the North Carolina man did become president.

Who was this man? Andrew Jackson. (Incidentally, this rift helped lead to the dual-party system, with Jackson, John C. Calhoun, and Martin Van Buren forming the Democratic Party, and Adams and Clay referred to as National Republicans.)

N★C Strange . . . but true

The VP Who Never Saw D.C.

Born in Sampson County in 1786, William Rufus Devane King seemed destined for great things. Rising in political circles, in 1852 he was elected vice president of the United States, to serve with President Franklin Pierce.

But King was sick with what was then called "consumption," tuberculosis. He traveled to Cuba for his health and there took the oath of office as vice president of the United States. His health continued to deteriorate, however, and King traveled to a plantation he owned in Alabama. He died in Alabama, having served a mere twenty-five days as vice president.

He is the only vice president who not only took the oath of office outside the United States, but never served a day of his office in Washington, D.C.

Power of the Written (and Read) Word

The little boy had nearly always felt inferior to kids his own age because of his secret. He dreaded anyone ever calling upon him to read, much less write, because it was nearly impossible for him. Born in Raleigh in 1808 to his impoverished parents, Jacob and Mary McDonough Johnson, his life took a turn for the worse when his father died. Although his mother remarried, the family remained poor, and at the age of ten, he was apprenticed to work in a tailor shop.

He was seventeen years old and well accomplished with needle and thread when the family moved to Greeneville, Tennessee. There he eventually set up his own tailor shop, but he remained illiterate.

Then the young man met a sixteen-year-old girl, Eliza McCardle. She fired his imagination with not only love but ambition. Eliza was well read, and after the two married in 1827, she began teaching her husband to read.

Night after night, when the tailor shop was closed and the chores were done, he labored over book and paper, learning to read and write.

Eliza taught her husband well, and he embarked on a political career that took him from mayor of the town to governor of Tennessee, then vice president to Abraham Lincoln. After Lincoln's assassination, he became the seventeenth president of the United States—Andrew Johnson.

The Infamous Misadventures of Nolichucky Jack

In the formative years of the United States, there were thirteen original states. But there was a fourteenth that no one would accept into the Union. This state went by the name Free Republic of Franklin, and its governor was a notorious politician—John Sevier, a man everyone knew as Nolichucky Jack because his home was near the Nolichucky River.

The Free Republic of Franklin existed for four short years (1784–1788), but during that time its existence and its governor's antics caused a great deal of political controversy and intrigue. Nolichucky Jack was for a time tempted to sign a treaty with Spain, a move that would have been disastrous for the still-emerging United States, and came close to declaring war against North Carolina—but that's getting ahead of the story.

The land in question was once a part of North Carolina. In the early 1780s, North Carolina's borders extended clear to the Mississippi River, but this didn't last long. After the Revolutionary War, many North Carolinians settled in the western boundaries of the then-wilderness lands of the Tarheel State. Many of those settlers then demanded that the government of North Carolina defend them from hostile natives and roving outlaws. Others in the state, however, were of the mind that those settlers were little better than the outlaws from which they demanded protection. Something had to be done, and Governor Alexander Martin was just the one to do it.

At Martin's urging, the North Carolina Assembly ceded the western lands back to the Continental Congress, for them to take care of the problems. This raised the ire of Nolichucky Jack. Already known as a fighting man who had made a name for himself in the Battle of Kings Mountain

during the War for Independence, he rounded up a few like-minded independent types and in 1784 they held a secession convention. They declared
three of North Carolina's counties—Greene, Sullivan, and Washington—to
be independent. They held a constitutional convention and named the
newly seceded counties the Free Republic of Franklin, after Benjamin
Franklin. Nolichucky Jack was elected governor.

Martin was infuriated at this political and geographical impertinence. He
said this was akin to treason, and sent word to Jack that he would send troops
to reclaim the counties as North Carolina's own. Jack responded in kind, saying he would (and could) quickly raise an army to defend this new republic.

To add to the chaos, a representative of the new republic, William
Cooke, arrived at the 1785 meeting of the Continental Congress, presenting
Franklin's petition for statehood. After the North Carolina delegation caught
its collective breath, it hotly debated such insurrection. A vote was taken,
which fell short by two for the republic to become admitted to the Union.

The Free Republic of Franklin endured an increasing amount of chaos.
For one thing, there was nothing to back Franklin's currency and the settlers
were obliged to barter for what they needed. Meanwhile, the North Carolina
Assembly tried to entice the people to return to the geographic fold by offering to waive all back taxes owed. Then Spain tried to get Jack to cooperate
in forming colonies in America (he declined).

Written records were confusing if not worthless. Marriage licenses, land
transactions, judicial decisions, and more were duplicated or reversed,
because North Carolina officials continued in these capacities even as the
Franklinite officials issued their own documents.

Finally, in November 1787, Congress handed down a decision that the
original claimant to a territory (in this case, North Carolina) could grant or
deny statehood to a territory within it that was petitioning for admission to
the Union. Naturally, North Carolina chose not to grant statehood to
Franklin, and the military of North Carolina seemed ready to swarm down
on the Franklinites. Jack petitioned Spain for help, but before Spain could
respond, a Tarheel named John Tipton and a group of law enforcement men

invaded Franklin, arrested Jack, and put him in jail. No sooner was he in jail than some of Jack's buddies from Franklin "busted him out" again, and took him back home.

Finally Jack and his Franklinites saw the futility in continuing with such a political tug-of-war. They surrendered and stood trial. Their punishment? They all had to take the Oath of Allegiance to the State of North Carolina.

When everything was calm again, the land that had been the Free Republic of Franklin was renamed the "Territory of the United States of America South of the Ohio River." From this came a new state, which we know today as Tennessee.

Its first governor? John Sevier, or Nolichucky Jack.

Guess Who? U.S. Census Bureau statistics list North Carolina as the eleventh most populous state. In 2000 census takers counted 8,049,313 residents in the Tarheel State.

Two "Rights" and a Wrong Choice

During the election year of 1844, Henry Clay came to Raleigh, campaigning for the office of president. He was very popular and thousands came to hear him give a speech at the state capitol. At the time, Texas was being considered for statehood, which Clay vehemently opposed.

Under the shade of an oak tree, Clay wrote what Raleigh historians refer to as "Clay's famous Texas letter." His letter warned that if the United States admitted Texas into the Union, the country would end up at war with Mexico. His advisors told him not to send the letter to the media, saying it would cost him the presidency. He is said to have retorted, "I would rather be right than president!" and mailed the letter.

He and his advisors both were right. The United States annexed Texas in 1845, went to war with Mexico the following year—and Clay lost the presidential race to James K. Polk, a North Carolinian.

The oak tree, dubbed "Henry Clay's oak," was later lost to disease, but the spot in downtown Raleigh where Clay wrote the famous letter is marked with a stone plaque.

Did You Know? This senator from Morganton was popular for his wit and good humor. He is best known for presiding as chairman of the Senate Select Committee on Presidential Campaign Activities during the infamous Watergate scandal of 1973, and often described himself as "a country lawyer."

Who was this senator? Sam Ervin.

Senator Jesse Helms's Secret for Longevity?

Forget health food stores when you're thinking about ways to live longer and better. Recently retired Senator Jesse Helms may be long-lived because of what is served in the Senate Cafeteria. *Slate* magazine attributed Helms's energy and longevity to this "famous Senate Bean Soup."

Senate Bean Soup

2 pounds dried navy beans (pea beans)

4 quarts hot water

1½ pounds smoked ham hocks

1 onion, chopped

2 tablespoons butter

Salt and pepper to taste

Wash and run hot water through the beans until they are slightly whitened. Place the beans in a large pot with the hot water. Add ham hocks and boil for 3 hours. Set aside to cool. Dice the ham and return to the soup. Lightly brown the chopped onion in butter and add to the soup. Before serving, bring to a boil, then season with salt and pepper. Serves 8.

N★C Stran©e . . . **but true**

The Gubernatorial Ghost

North Carolina is chock-full of ghosts and ghost stories, and that even goes for the governor's mansion. Raleigh historian Parker Call says the ghost is believed to be the spirit of Governor Daniel Fowle, the first governor to live in the mansion. Fowle had brought his own furniture to the mansion, including his bed.

"Unfortunately, he only lived in the mansion three months before he died, but his bed remained in the house," explains Call. "In the 1960s when Bob Scott became governor, he was a large man and couldn't sleep in that bed. He asked that it be moved and replaced with a larger bed that would accommodate him. When Fowle's bed was moved, the mansion began to be disturbed with mysterious knocking sounds. People still think it is the spirit of Daniel Fowle, letting them know he doesn't appreciate his bed being moved from the executive sleeping chambers."

Some say the executive mansion in Raleigh is haunted by the first governor who lived and died there, Daniel Fowle. (PHOTO BY THE AUTHOR)

N★C POLITICAL TRIVIA

Q. Who came as a surveyor to Gates County, surveyed the area, formed a company to drain part of the Dismal Swamp, and bought a tract of land in the county?

A. George Washington.

Q. Who was the first woman in the nation to be appointed to the position of postmistress?

A. Sarah DeCrow was appointed on September 27, 1792, in Hertford.

Q. What was the name detractors gave the Safe Storage of Firearms bill, introduced into the House of Representatives in April 2001?

A. Home Invaders Protection Act.

Q. Until October 2001, at what age could a girl get married in North Carolina without parental or guardian consent?

A. On October 1, the minimum marriage age was raised from twelve to fourteen.

Q. In 1866 a law was passed prohibiting what activity in the halls of the Davie County Courthouse?

A. Horseback riding in the hallways.

Q. How many representatives are there in the North Carolina State Legislature?

A. 120.

Q. What president established the Appalachian Regional Commission to improve the lives and prospects of the people in this area?

A. President John F. Kennedy.

Q. What thirteen states are now part of this commission?

A. North Carolina, South Carolina, Tennessee, Georgia, Alabama, Kentucky, Maryland, Pennsylvania, Virginia, West Virginia, New York, Mississippi, and Ohio.

Q. What is the "youngest" county in North Carolina, created in 1911?

A. Avery County.

Q. How many counties are in North Carolina?

A. Exactly 100.

Q. Who was the first woman to be named to a post by the Reagan administration of 1980?

A. Elizabeth Hanford Dole, born in Salisbury, became assistant to the president for public liaison.

3
Planes, Trains, and Automobiles

Warping, Rudders, and Mosquitoes

The two men were drawn to this Outer Banks village. Despite the mosquitoes that one described as coming "in a mighty cloud . . . darkening the sun," and causing "extreme misery," the two were determined to spend time here. It was, they agreed, the perfect place for what they had in mind. It was extremely isolated. It had fair breezes. The uncluttered beaches stretched for miles and were at least one mile wide. And the people of the town, although somewhat suspicious of their motives, at least put up with what was considered eccentric, somewhat bizarre behavior.

What surprised the two were the unexpected squalls that came up several times weekly, forcing them to hold their tent down in the night to keep it from blowing away. Between the squalls and "bone-chilling cold" temperatures at night, it was a wonder either of them wanted to ever return to this exotic but forbidding place.

But return they did, determined to work with the elements and each other. Engineers primarily, the two had chosen a place near Kitty Hawk as the place to solve the mystery of flight and prove, once and for all, that heavier-than-air transportation was possible.

For several years the problem of balance had stumped brothers Orville and Wilbur Wright. Then they added a warp—a helical twist applied across the entire wing of the plane—that would control balance in flight. This problem had hindered the efforts of Germany's Otto Lilienthal and other aeronautical pioneers. Modifying the rudder helped with control and added lift.

Finally, in twelve seconds and with Orville at the controls of the machine named the *Flyer*, the possibility of manned flight was proven and history was changed. It had taken years of struggles with squalls, mosquitoes, and engineering frustrations, but because of the determination of two brothers from Dayton, Ohio, the first airplane flew 120 feet in the air above the sand dunes near Kill Devil Hills, on December 17, 1903. The jubilant brothers made three more attempts at flight on that historic day, with the longest flight lasting fifty-nine seconds and covering 852 feet (further flights were not possible because the plane was damaged by a sudden gust).

The *Flyer* that became airborne on that historic day is now on display at the Smithsonian in Washington, D.C.

N★C Stran©e . . . but true

How Technology Changed the History Records

Most people believe that the historic first flight took place in Kitty Hawk. This is not exactly true, despite what the history books say.

The day the brothers made their historic first flight at Kill Devil Hills, five miles south of Kitty Hawk, they were justifiably euphoric and wanted to share the news with their father. The only way to get word to him was by telegraph, and the nearest telegraph station was in Kitty Hawk.

Thus, with a telegraphed message datelined Kitty Hawk and not Kill Devil Hills, technology changed the way this historical event was recorded for posterity.

Did You Know? Every December 17 for more than forty years, the Man Will Never Fly Society has met in Kitty Hawk. It's no coincidence that they meet on the anniversary of the first manned flight of Orville and Wilbur Wright. Saying that the Wright brothers faked that flight by using a bicycle to pull the airplane, the primary agenda of the members of this society is just having a good time on the ground. Al Jones, spokesperson for the society, admits that some of the members arrive by airplane for the convention.

America's "First Airplane"

In 2002 students in the carpentry class at the Roanoke-Chowan Community College in Ahoskie were busy working on an airplane. Not just any airplane—a replica of what they say is America's first airplane, built by James Henry Gatling in 1873 (you can read about his brother, Richard Gatling, in Chapter 10).

Students at Roanoke-Chowan Community College built a replica of the 1873 James Henry Gatling Airplane, which they claim is American's first airplane. (COURTESY MURFREESBORO HISTORICAL ASSOCIATION)

Thomas C. Parramore, Ph.D., North Carolina aviation historian, says that although the original Gatling airplane failed to fly, some features of it were embodied in the Wright airplane that did fly in 1903. Completed for the hundredth anniversary celebration of the Wright brothers' first flight, the replica is permanently located in Murfreesboro's Historic District.

The Bumblebee That Didn't Quite Fly

Born in 1869 and growing up in Core Sound, William Luther Paul was fascinated with how things worked, and as a teenager was known as "Mr. Fix It."

Paul was fascinated with flight and the strides made to achieve manned flight. In 1903 he built his own flying machine, an experimental helicopter he named *The Bumble Bee*. He tested it in a makeshift wind tunnel, an open-ended barn, and found that *The Bumble Bee* could achieve lift as high as five feet carrying sixty pounds of ballast.

Of course, later that same year, the Wright brothers made their historic first flights. This, combined with Paul's wife's concern for his safety and a lack of funds, prompted him to abandon his work on *The Bumble Bee*.

He and his family moved to Beaufort in 1911 and Luther continued to work on his inventions (he is credited with building one of Carteret County's first automobiles). He was also involved in making motion pictures, and when in the 1920s he wrote Thomas Edison about collaborating on a "talking-motion picture" project, Edison responded saying he was too busy.

Paul died in 1946, but a model of the original experimental helicopter is on display at the Beaufort Historical Association. It was built by Luther Paul's grandson, Grayden Paul Jr.

Operation Bumble Bee

In the post–World War II years of 1946 to 1948, the U.S. government chose Topsail Island as a site to test secret missiles. Termed Operation Bumble Bee, the goal of the project was to develop a supersonic missile that could reach an air target at a range of ten to twenty miles.

The project, one of the earliest developments of the U.S. missile program, used facilities at nearby Camp Davis in Holly Ridge to accommodate five hundred personnel. The missile test range was built in a year, and was one of the best-equipped facilities in the country.

From the research conducted during Operation Bumble Bee, more than one triumphant development emerged. Operation Bumble Bee provided technology that allowed U.S. warships to carry onboard missiles with enhanced ability to destroy enemy aircraft. In addition, the Ramjet Engine was developed, which is now the basis for all jet aircraft.

Buildings that remain from Operation Bumble Bee have been designated as historical sites in the National Register of Historic Places, and now the formerly top-secret area is open to the public.

The Comeback Train

When the logging industry became a major source of income for the people of western North Carolina in the 1890s, transporting men, tools, and logs was a problem. Most locomotives of the day couldn't climb the steep

Once an abandoned logging rail line, the Great Smoky Mountains Railroad is now one of the main attractions of western North Carolina. (COURTESY N.C. DIVISION OF TOURISM, FILM, AND SPORTS DEVELOPMENT)

grades of the area. To hold traction on the rails placed so hastily in the region, two types of locomotives, the Shay and the Clima, were used. The Shay had increased traction because of its vertical cylinders, placed to the right of an off-set boiler, and the Clima also had a vertical drive gear. These trains ran between Dillsboro and Murphy on a rail line owned by the Norfolk Southern Railroad.

Until the Great Smoky Mountains National Park was established in 1934, the Shay and the Clima ruled the land, as did the logger. Once the park was established and set aside as a wilderness area and people began to travel primarily by highways, the railroad lost its usefulness. In 1988 increasing maintenance costs and decreasing traffic obliged the Norfolk Southern to abandon the Dillsboro-Murphy line.

The line was saved from possible destruction by the quick action of the state of North Carolina. It purchased the line and leased it to a group of shippers and investors, incorporated as the Great Smoky Mountains Railroad and based in Dillsboro.

Now the locomotives, with an additional locomotive, a Baldwin, give passengers entertaining rides on a fifty-three-mile route from Dillsboro to Andrews and Murphy. The Baldwin has a history of its own—it was a World War II locomotive and "starred" in the movie *This Property Is Condemned*, with Charles Bronson, Robert Redford, and Natalie Wood. The cars the locomotives pull have been used on various other lines and have poetic names such as the Silver Meteor and Dixie Flyer. Besides having entertainment value, the line services the agricultural, business, and industrial needs of the three cities.

The abandoned logging rail line nobody wanted has become one of the main attractions of western North Carolina.

Did You Know? One of the most photographed railroad stations in the United States is in the tiny town of Hamlet. It's the circa-1900 depot originally belonging to the old Seaboard Air Line Railway, now used as the National Railroad Museum and Hall of Fame.

Along This "Train" of Thought

In 1866 the East Tennessee and Western North Carolina Railroad Company built a railroad that ran from Johnson City, Tennessee, to iron mines in Cranberry, North Carolina. The narrow-gauge line began running in 1881, and in 1916 it was extended to Boone and transported lumber and passengers between the cities. The train, dubbed "Tweetsie" by the locals for its shrill whistle, became a part of mountain life.

Like trains elsewhere, Tweetsie's livelihood was adversely affected by the construction of highways, and in 1950 the railroad company met its demise. Some railroad enthusiasts purchased Tweetsie Locomotive Number 12 and moved her to Virginia, where they planned to put her back on track. Hurricane Hazel destroyed the railroad tracks, however, so the discouraged rail buffs had to sell the locomotive.

Famous singing cowboy Gene Autry bought her from the Virginians, supposedly to feature her in Western films. Somehow, a North Carolina native named Grover Robbins Jr. talked the movie legend into selling him Tweetsie Number 12 for the sum of one dollar—so she could come back home to the mountains. Robbins brought Tweetsie to his hometown of Blowing Rock, and had her restored by expert train-repair folks in Hickory.

Tweetsie made her tourist debut just a few miles away from the old railroad depot in Boone, along with some of the original rail cars, also restored in Hickory. Now the legend of the coal-fired steam train lives on as Tweetsie transports delighted families, once again sounding her shrill, cheerful whistle through the hills and valleys of the Blue Ridge Mountains. Once in danger of the scrap heap, Tweetsie enjoys life anew and is listed on the National Register of Historic Places.

The Man Who Transformed Commercial Transportation

Born in Maxton, trucker Malcolm P. McLean got his start hauling barrels of tobacco. He must have been an extraordinarily observant man, for he noted the problems inherent with the way goods were shipped. As late as the early 1950s, goods were transferred using cargo nets, but loose cargoes often suffered damage in transit and pilferage occurred, causing insurance rates for cargo carriers to skyrocket. McLean also noticed that it took truckers and dock workers far too long to load and offload cargo.

Then McLean had an idea: get rid of cargo nets and pack the goods into boxes. He experimented with large boxes he called containers and in 1956 converted an old World War II tanker, *The Ideal X*, into the first container ship. On its maiden voyage, the old tanker successfully transported fifty-eight containers from Port Newark, New Jersey, to Houston, Texas. The shipping world took note and realized McLean's "boxes" would decrease insurance rates and increase the speed and safety of shipments. Observers also noted the speed with which McLean's company offloaded cargo, using Gantry cranes instead of the hands and backs of longshoremen.

The trucker-turned-shipping-magnate named his infant company Sea-Land Service. McLean's company became the world's largest container shipping service, and at least 90 percent of today's cargo is shipped in containers. Malcolm P. McLean died in May 2001, but will always be remembered as the "Father of Containerization."

Did You Know? The world's most complicated bridge is the Linn Cove Viaduct around the base of Grandfather Mountain, on the

Blue Ridge Parkway near Linville. It's internationally famous because it is an engineering marvel, with so many complicated curves that each fifty-ton segment was constructed one at a time. Each segment is unlike any other piece on the bridge, and the entire bridge has only one straight segment.

The Linn Cove Viaduct around the base of Grandfather Mountain is the world's most complicated bridge. (COURTESY N.C. DIVISION OF TOURISM, FILM, AND SPORTS DEVELOPMENT)

Wagons, Ho!

A two-hour drive along the crest of the Unicoi Mountains takes you over the Cherohala Skyway, a lovely, winding two-lane road that connects western North Carolina to eastern Tennessee. The road, completed in 1996, carries travelers past cascading waterfalls, wilderness areas, and hiking trails. It also boasts, among other natural attractions, Joyce Kilmer Memorial Forest. It took the vision of a local Kiwanis Club group to foster sufficient interest for this road to see completion.

It all started in the 1950s in nearby Tellico Plains, Tennessee, where some residents complained that the roads to North Carolina were so bad, they might as well be traveling by wagon train. The comments sparked the local Kiwanis Club members, led by local historian Charles Hall, to organize a wagon train to generate media attention (and thereby funds) to build a sure-enough highway from Tellico Plains to Robbinsville. The first wagon trains left Tellico Plains for North Carolina in June 1958 with nearly seventy wagons and more than three hundred riders on horseback. The event gained media attention and did, indeed, generate funds for a highway.

The Kiwanis Club members and others decided not to stop with one wagon train; it became an almost annual event until the highway was nearly completed. Even though the opening ceremonies for the highway were held in October 1996, some people still get together for the wagon train event, usually around the first weekend in July.

Did You Know? The Cherohala Skyway was named by Charles Hall, who combined the names of two forests the highway spans: the Cherokee National Forest on the Tennessee side and the Nantahala National Forest in North Carolina. At the Unicoi Crest overlook (elevation 4,470 feet), you can see three states: Tennessee from the west, North Carolina in the east, and Georgia to the southwest. Look for equally breathtaking vistas around the Santeetlah area (elevation 5,390 feet).

The Road to Nowhere

Just north of Bryson City and near the quiet village of Townsend, Tennessee, deep in the woods bordering Fontana Lake, is a road that ends abruptly at a long tunnel that traverses underground for several hundred yards.

The road is formally known as Lakeview Drive, but the locals know it as the Road to Nowhere. It was begun in the late 1950s as a combined project of the U.S. Department of the Interior, the Tennessee Valley Authority, and Swain County. Lakeview Drive was intended to bring more visitors to Fontana Lake, and provide a more straightforward route from Bryson City to Townsend. Because of a lack of foresight, however, problems got in the way.

Twenty-eight family cemeteries were in the road's path, and people weren't willing to move their beloveds' remains. That, plus concerns about the environmental impact the road would create for the pristine wilderness around it, halted the building of the road.

You can drive most of the road in the wilderness at the North Carolina–Tennessee border, and when it comes to an end, you can explore the tunnel on foot. Both the road and the tunnel remain as mute witness to our sometimes shortsighted ambitions.

N★C TRANSPORTATION TRIVIA

Q. In what North Carolina county was the hot-air balloon made that was used by Tracy Barnes, the first person to travel across the United States in a hot-air balloon?

A. Iredell County (The Balloon Works).

Q. How did High Point, North Carolina, come by its name?

A. The town was founded on the highest point of land on the railroad that ran between Goldsboro and Charlotte.

Q. How many miles of highway does the state maintain?

A. At last count, seventy-six thousand miles—making it the largest state highway system in the United States.

Q. What is the name of the oldest known working tugboat? (Hint: when not on duty, it's located at Manteo's Salty Dog Marina.)

A. *The Lookout.*

Q. What is the name of the stretch of two-lane road that, from the state line at Deals Gap going north toward Maryville, Tennessee, contains 318 curves in only eleven miles of highway?

A. The aptly named and nationally famous "Tail of the Dragon," U.S. Highway 129.

Q. What do locals call the stretch of U.S. 158 between Elizabeth City and Fort Raleigh?

A. The Virginia Dare Trail.

Q. What North Carolina city is the site of the largest display in the southeast of old work boats?

A. Wilmington.

Q. What year did work on the Blue Ridge Parkway begin?

A. 1935.

Before the War

The Paul Revere of the South

In the early days of America's independence, twenty-seven delegates met at the Charlotte Courthouse and voted "Aye" on making Mecklenburg County independent from England. That day, May 20, 1775, Captain James Jack took the job of carrying copies of the resolution to the president of the Continental Congress and to the three North Carolina representatives.

In Salisbury, when Jack stopped to read the proclamation to the court in session, most of the people in earshot reacted with wild cheering—except for two lawyers who wanted to hold Jack and charge him with treason. The lawyers' objections were overruled and Jack continued on his mission.

In all, Jack rode more than five hundred miles, beset by either enthusiastic approval or threats of violence. As legend has it, he arrived on June 23, 1775, in Philadelphia to present the resolution. Upon his arrival he was dismayed to learn of Congress's plans to make an official statement to the King of England, denying Mecklenburg's request for independence.

Incensed, he is quoted as saying to those gathered there, "Gentlemen, you may debate here about 'reconciliation' and memorialize your king, but bear in mind, Mecklenburg owes no allegiance to, and is separated from, the crown of Great Britain forever."

Of course you know that separation of the colonies from Britain was imminent. Although he was perhaps a bit ahead of his time, Captain James Jack is still regarded as the Paul Revere of the South.

Tea and Taxes

The coastal village of Edenton saw the first political action by women in the American colonies. On October 26, 1774, the ladies of Edenton and five nearby counties gathered at the home of Penelope Barker. They shared tea and wrote a declaration against the high taxes levied against American colonists by the English throne.

The document they signed eventually made its way to the British newspaper, the *Morning Chronicle & London Advertiser*, which voiced editorial disapproval of women's involvement in politics. After hearing of the ladies' patriotic stance, citizens in both the Carolinas and Georgia were inspired to swear off tea in opposition to the tax levied by the British. As a result, casks of tea sat unconsumed in warehouses in Charleston.

When the Revolution broke out and patriots gained control of Charleston, they sold the casks of tea to help finance the war effort!

The Days When Lawyers Were Revered

There are lots of jokes about lawyers these days, but in North Carolina, the American Revolution was led by barristers. North Carolina's own Declaration of Independence, known as the Halifax Resolves, was written by an attorney. Most of the members of the first Continental Congress (which included Tarheels) were also attorneys, as were twenty-one of fifty-six signers of the Declaration of Independence.

Next time you want to tell a joke about lawyers, consider going *out* of state to do it.

The Tale of the Overmountain Men

The Continental Army surrendered the city of Charleston, South Carolina, to the British on May 12, 1780. Before this, the army had been devastated by defeats at the battles of Cowpens and Waxhaws. The Continental Army was demoralized and things did not look good for the colonies. But no one realized how feisty the colonists in North Carolina could be.

North Carolina was the last bastion between the invading British general, Charles Cornwallis, and his final destination. Virginia was the largest colony in the Americas, and Cornwallis was determined to take it because this would bring the struggle for independence to a dismal and disheartening close. He, too, underestimated the fierce independent nature of the mountain men of the Tarheel State.

The Continental Army was in disarray, and settlers in the mountain region of North Carolina heeded the call to arms to fight for America's independence. They were mostly farmers, hunters, and trappers by trade, most with no military experience whatsoever. So untrained were they that the British referred to them as "mongrels," and the invading Brits threatened that if the Americans did not submit to British rule, they would "lay waste the country with fire and sword." This, too, did nothing to dissuade the Tarheel mountain men.

Seeing their numbers grow, other civilian soldiers from southern Virginia and Tennessee joined the ranks of the soldiers now known as the Overmountain Men. In a late fall campaign to stop the British from getting to Virginia, the patriots (including Daniel Boone) marched 313 miles, gathering forces as they went through four states, hot on the trail of their foe. More soldiers from Georgia joined the Overmountain Men in Polk County; then they met and defeated the British in the decisive Battle of Kings Mountain. In just one day—October 7, 1780—the farmer soldiers won a pivotal battle for their beloved America.

> *Did You Know?* The nation's oldest Revolutionary War drama, entitled *Horn in the West,* depicts Daniel Boone and the Battle of Kings Mountain and is held in Boone every summer. Also, the pivotal victory of patriot militia over the British Loyalist forces is commemorated at Kings Mountain National Military Park in Cleveland County.

Losing the Battle, Winning the War

The Battle of Guilford Courthouse on March 15, 1781, may be officially recorded as a loss for the colonies, but in the long run, it wasn't. Here's why.

General Charles Cornwallis had mounted his second attack on North Carolina in January 1781. General Nathanael Greene had always stayed a step ahead of the invading British, trying to keep himself and his soldiers strategically situated between Cornwallis and his supplies in South Carolina. As Cornwallis advanced, Greene retreated; this forced Cornwallis to begin abandoning supplies to make pursuit easier on his troops.

When Greene got Cornwallis as far as 230 miles from his South Carolina supplies, he took a stand at the Guilford County Courthouse. Cornwallis's side suffered badly. At the end of the fighting, the colonists had 78 dead and 183 wounded, compared to 93 British dead and 439 wounded.

Greene retreated to save his remaining men, and although Cornwallis continued his attempt to defeat the patriots, he and his men had been badly weakened and were ill supplied, thanks to Greene's ingenious maneuvers. The British were ultimately defeated by General George Washington and General Jean Baptiste de Vimeur, Comte de Rochambeau in Yorktown, Virginia, in October 1781. Today, when you visit the Guilford County Courthouse in Greensboro, you will know that a quick-witted patriot made sure that, although Cornwallis technically won that battle, he effectively lost the war.

At the time of the battle, the town was named Martinsborough. It was renamed Greensboro in honor of Greene, and Guilford Courthouse National Military Park is the nation's first Revolutionary War military park.

The Old-Name Game

See if you can guess what these Native American names used for towns, rivers, or forests mean in English. Match 'em up!

1. Nantahala	A. Slow-moving turtle
2. Tuckasegee	B. Land of the noon-day sun
3. Cataloochee	C. Place of the sweet bay tree
4. Scuppernong River	D. Wave upon wave
5. Pasquotank	E. Land of beautiful women
6. Perquimans	F. Where the currents divide

Answers:

1. (B) Nantahala Gorge is so deep that early Native Americans said that the sun shone into it only during the sun's zenith, at noon.

2. (A) The Tuckasegee River can move slowly in places, especially around Bryson City. The early Cherokee described its movement as slow, like a turtle, probably naming it where they observed it flowing in the Bryson City area.

3. (D) Cataloochee Ranch is in Maggie Valley, and from here it looks as though the mountains are huge waves, rolling toward you in the mist. Other places carry the "cataloochee" name: Cataloochee Valley, Cataloochee River, and Cataloochee Ski Area.

4. (C) Scuppernong is an Algonquin word. The Indians named the area around the Scuppernong River, which runs through Tyrell County, for the many bay trees there. Also growing in the area is a grape in the muscadine family, which is used to make a local wine, and the name "scuppernong" was given to this grape by a naturalist in 1810. However, this grape is not related to the bay tree.

5. (F) Elizabeth City is on the Pasquotank River, in Pasquotank County. Explorers and settlers came here as early as 1585—long before Jamestown and Plymouth Rock.

6. (E) Perquimans is the name of a county, taken from a Yeopin Indian word. Unfortunately, the legend behind the name has not survived the years. (When asked if the name describes the county's present inhabitants, Sid Ealy, director of the Chamber of Commerce, replied, "You'll all just have to come see for yourselves!")

The Capital of Raleigh and "Cherry Bounce"

The Joel Lane House in Raleigh, which dates back to 1760, is not only the oldest existing building in Wake County, but is also part of an amusing story relating to the establishment of Raleigh as the permanent state capital.

Before Raleigh received this designation in 1792, the state capital had been moved many times. Edenton was first (1708 into the 1740s); followed by Bath (in the 1740s); Wilmington (later in the 1740s); New Bern (off and on between the 1740s and 1790s); Hillsborough, Halifax, and Tarboro (between 1770 and the 1780s); and then Fayetteville (1780s). The people of North Carolina probably breathed one huge sigh of relief when everyone voted on making Raleigh the permanent state capital.

These facts you can find in virtually any North Carolina history book. While you can still visit the Joel Lane House, here's "the rest of the story" that you *won't* find in any history book, from docent LeRae Umfleet.

Raleigh didn't exist until it was founded as the state capital. As a matter of fact, there wasn't a single town in Wake County until Raleigh's founding. The state of North Carolina wanted to choose a new capital in the middle of the state, making it easier for everyone to travel to the capital for business. The previous state capitals had all been on the coast and were inaccessible for people in the mountains and the Piedmont areas. Wake County was close to the geographical center of the state, so the real decision was where in Wake County to put the capital.

The committee agreed on a general location within ten miles of Isaac Hunter's tavern, a popular stopping place. Several men, including Joel Lane, offered to sell the state's representatives land in the ten-mile stretch from Hunter's tavern. The committee reviewed the land offerings and decided to settle it with a vote. During the deliberations, Lane entertained the representatives at his home.

The first two votes on a Thursday in March were inconclusive, with no clear majority. They decided to adjourn and vote again the next day. This is when Lane worked his magic.

Oral tradition holds that he entertained his guests with a bountiful table and free-flowing spirits such as Cherry Bounce, a sort of cherry cordial and whiskey concoction. There is no agreed-upon historic recipe for the drink but with each iteration of the tale, the brew has become ever more potent. The guests reportedly enjoyed a serving (or more) of Cherry Bounce.

Next morning, when the guests' collective fog lifted, they offered to buy a thousand acres from Lane for the site of the new state capital. It was named Raleigh in honor of Sir Walter Raleigh, the English explorer whose exploits led to the colonization of North Carolina in the seventeenth century.

Joel Lane's reputation has descended through history as a man who was an outgoing, well-mannered individual who used his influence and wealth to secure the location of the city of Raleigh in what was, literally, his front yard. His home is preserved and furnished as it was when he lived there and is open for tours led by costumed docents.

It's worth a visit—with or without being served the famous (or infamous) drink. If you do want to work your own Cherry Bounce magic, try this recipe suggested by LaRae Umfleet, who says the drink improves with age and is "much better when it's two to three years old."

The famous "Cherry Bounce" drink worked its magic at the Joel Lane House, and Raleigh was unanimously voted the capital of North Carolina. (Photo by the author)

Cherry Bounce

4 quarts cherries, drained

2 quarts sugar

1 quart best whiskey or brandy

Stir together cherries and sugar and let stand overnight. In the morning, stir again and add whiskey or brandy. Store in a stone jar, put on a lid, and seal the edges with a cloth dipped in paraffin. Let stand for 6 weeks, squeeze out juices, and strain and filter it.

N★C Strange . . . but true

The executive mansion in Raleigh is a stunning piece of architecture, with brickwork on the surrounding walkways. Many of the bricks have people's signatures on them, but these signed bricks do not represent donations as you might think. When the mansion was being built, the inmates at the state penitentiary were the ones to make these bricks. Every day, they signed their names on the first brick they made, and at the end of the day they signed their last brick. When you walk around the executive mansion today, take note of all the different signatures, many quite ornate in their script.

Some Early Settlers

In the early 1700s a group of Siouan-speaking Indians settled in what is now Robeson, Hoke, and Scotland counties. Growing and thriving, they were first referred to as Cheraws, then were thought to be Croatan, then in 1911 the North Carolina General Assembly changed their name to simply the "Indians of Robeson County." At one time they were also thought to be a part of the Cherokee nation, but their origin in still unclear. Finally, in 1956 the U.S. Congress recognized them as the Lumbees.

The Lumbee people have made many contributions. They helped defend this country, starting with the Revolutionary War. In 1887 the Lumbee people built Croatan Indian Normal School, today the University of North Carolina at Pembroke. They opened the first Indian-owned bank in the United States, the Lumbee Bank in Pembroke. It is the only tribe in this country to hold on to its native lands, without being forced onto a reservation.

Town Names, Now and Then

Here are some North Carolina towns' original names, and their names as you know them today. See if you can match them up.

Now	Then
1. Robbins	A. Elkville
2. Buladean	B. Huckleberry Swamp
3. Enfield	C. Pea Landing
4. Windsor	D. Shallop's Landing
5. Atlantic	E. Gray's Landing
6. Williamston	F. Campbellton/Cross Creek
7. Connelly Springs	G. Martinsborough
8. Greenville	H. Excelsior
9. Fayetteville	I. Skewarky
10. Columbia	J. Hunting Quarters
11. Calabash	K. Magnetic City
12. Ferguson	L. Mechanicsville

Answers: 1. (L) 2. (K) 3. (B) 4. (E) 5. (J) 6. (I) 7. (H) 8. (G) 9 (F) 10. (D) 11. (C) 12. (A)

When a Tarheel "Saved" George Washington

In 1814 when the British were attacking the city of Washington, D.C., they were bent on burning down President James Madison's home. Hearing of their intentions and knowing that everything in the home would be destroyed, the president's wife, Dolley, gathered what possessions she could as she prepared to flee the city.

Born Dorothea Payne from Guilford County, Dolley quickly saw that one thing in the home could never be replaced: a large portrait of George Washington in a splendid frame. Realizing that there was no time to unscrew the painting from the wall, she ordered that the frame be broken and the canvas be removed.

The Redcoats arrived within minutes of her evacuation, looting and burning the house, and leaving only the charred shell of the executive mansion in their destructive wake.

Because of a Tarheel with steel in her spine, the only original piece to survive from the executive mansion (later to be known as the White House) is that portrait of George Washington she saved August 24, 1814. A replica of this painting by Gilbert Stuart hangs in the East Room of the White House today. The original that Dolley saved is on display in the Smithsonian's National Portrait Gallery.

Dolley Madison is the only first lady born in North Carolina. Her accomplishments are honored in exhibits at the Greensboro Historical Museum.

Dolley Madison is the only first lady born in North Carolina. When the British burned the executive mansion in 1814, she had the presence of mind to rescue the portrait of George Washington. (LIBRARY OF CONGRESS)

Unusual Town Names

Some towns in North Carolina have strange names, with sometimes off-beat reasons for their naming.

★ **Kill Devil Hills:** Early white settlers regularly imbibed a rum drink said to be strong enough to kill the devil himself.

★ **Lizard Lick:** One early resident regularly took his stroll alongside a local fence, knocking (or "licking") the lizards off the fence railing with his cane as he passed.

★ **Cats Square:** Unwanted cats were abandoned there.

★ **Old Trap:** This town in Camden County was originally given the derisive name of The Trap by "decent" women up in arms over the number of taverns and loose women in the area.

★ **Pigeonroost:** Passenger pigeons, now extinct, once roosted there.

★ **Boogertown:** People who made moonshine kept the curious away by letting it be thought that evil spirits, or "boogers," hid in the woods.

★ **Rabbit Shuffle:** Early settlers of this town in Caswell County thought the soil quality was so poor that even a rabbit had to shuffle to get sustenance.

★ **Machelhe Island:** This island on the Pasquotank River was named from the first two letters of each of the owner's four children (Mary, Charles, Eloise, and Helen).

An Accident Leads to an Invention

George Gist, the son of a woman from a prominent Cherokee family and a fur trader from Virginia, was hunting in the area of North Carolina that is now the Cherokee Nation. He had a hunting accident that forced him into a period of inactivity, and during this time, became fascinated with the marks white people made on paper. He called the papers "talking leaves," because he saw how people could communicate using a written language. Gist then decided he would create a written language and started working on one for the Cherokee language. He labored for more than ten years to create the eighty-five-character syllabary, using characters to represent syllables rather than individual letters. This was adopted by the Cherokee Nation in 1821 and became the basis for the written Cherokee language. Using this syllabary, the Cherokee people established their first newspaper, the *Cherokee Phoenix*. That paper no longer

George Gist, better known as Sequoyah, invented the Cherokee syllabary. (COURTESY TENNESSEE TOURIST DEVELOPMENT)

exists, but the *Cherokee One Feather*, an English language newspaper, is published weekly out of Cherokee, North Carolina.

Because of that accident and forced inactivity, Gist, known better as Sequoyah, helped preserve an entire culture through the first written language of native North America. Now a bust of his likeness stands at the entrance to the Museum of the Cherokee Indian in Cherokee.

N★C BEFORE THE WAR TRIVIA

Q. During the Tuscarora War, where did approximately 950 Indians lose their lives?

A. Nooherooka.

Q. What was North Carolina's first military school, established in Williamsboro in 1826?

A. Bingham School.

Q. What four states border North Carolina?

A. Tennessee, Virginia, Georgia, and South Carolina.

Q. What town hosts the Annual Soldiers' Reunion Celebration, the oldest patriotic event of its kind?

A. Newton.

Q. What is the motto of North Carolina?

A. The Latin phrase, *Esse quam videri,* which means, "To be, rather than to seem."

Q. From what author was this quote derived?

A. Cicero, in his essay on friendship, *De Amicitia*.

Q. What Revolutionary War hero was such a colorful character that Wayne County was named in his honor?

A. "Mad Anthony" Wayne.

Q. *What beautifully restored building in New Bern was the home of the first British colonial governor when the town served as the colony's capital in 1770?*

A. *Tryon Palace, named after British governor William Tryon. Following the Revolutionary War, Tryon Palace became the first capital of the independent state of North Carolina.*

(COURTESY TRYON PALACE HISTORIC SITES AND GARDENS)

Q. What bordering colony so hotly contested the boundary with North Carolina that an official survey in 1728 was required to settle the dispute?

A. Virginia.

Q. When did North Carolina enter the Union?

A. November 21, 1789.

Q. When Sir Robert Heath was granted land from Albemarle Sound southward to Florida in 1629 and named it "Carolina," who was he naming it after?

A. King Charles I (Carolina is the Latin form of Charles).

Q. When were the Carolinas split into North and South, and why?

A. In 1663 King Charles II realized the area was too large to be managed efficiently and put eight "Lords Proprietors" in charge of what became referred to as North Carolina and South Carolina.

Q. What courthouse is the oldest still in use?

A. The Chowan County Courthouse, circa 1767.

Q. What three North Carolinians signed the Declaration of Independence, adopted by Congress on July 4, 1776?

A. William Hooper, Joseph Hewes, and John Penn.

Q. When did the North Carolina Legislature charter the University of North Carolina?

A. In 1789, making it the first state university in the United States.

Q. What Spanish explorer in 1540 came looking for gold in what are now Jackson, Cherokee, and Clay counties?

A. Hernando de Soto.

Q. In what year was the oldest recorded land deal in North Carolina?

A. In 1661, between Yeopin Indians and George Durant, in Hertford.

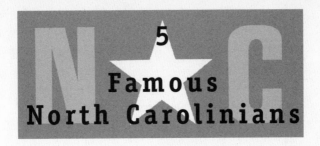

5

Famous North Carolinians

The "Barefoot Contessa" from the Tarheel State

The Barefoot Contessa was one of the movies that starred Ava Gardner and contributed to her enduring fame. Born December 25, 1922, in a rural area outside Smithfield, Ava Lavinia Gardner was one of eight children in the family of Jonas and Mary Gardner. To help make ends meet, little Ava's parents ran a boardinghouse for teachers of the rural Brodgen School, and the children often lent a hand.

After graduating from Rock Ridge High School in 1939, Ava went on to take secretarial courses at Atlantic Christian College in Wilson. She had completed her first year of study there when she visited her sister, Beatrice, and Beatrice's husband, Larry Tarr, a professional photographer in New York City. During that visit he took photos of Ava and displayed one on the wall of his studio. Someone saw her photo on the wall, and Ava was "discovered"—she was invited to do a screen test with Metro-Goldwyn-Mayer Studios and signed her first movie contract in 1941.

She later married actor Mickey Rooney, then swing-band leader Artie Shaw, and finally singer Frank Sinatra, but all of her marriages ended in divorce. She remained friends with each ex-husband throughout her life, and though she had no children, enjoyed close relationships with her nieces and nephews.

Ava Gardner was born in a rural area outside Smithfield. (COURTESY JOHNSTON COUNTY VISITORS BUREAU)

When she was thirty-three, Ava moved to Spain, where she lived for eight years; she then lived in London for twenty-six years until her death in 1990. She is remembered for many wonderful films, including *One Touch of Venus*.

But that's not the whole story about Ava Gardner. In 1939 an attractive secretarial student in Wilson had happened to kiss a twelve-year-old boy on the cheek. Two years later, the boy opened a newspaper and saw a photo of the face he couldn't forget, in an article about Ava's marriage to Mickey Rooney. Only then did Tom Banks learn the name of the beautiful girl who had kissed him.

The young man later became a doctor and married. He and his wife, Lorraine, spent much of their time collecting memorabilia relating to the beautiful actress. In the early 1980s, Banks bought the house where a young Ava and her family had lived in Smithfield, and for nine years he operated the Ava Gardner Museum in her former home.

Banks died of a stroke in August 1989 at the museum and, coincidentally, Gardner died in London of a stroke the following January. Lorraine Banks donated the collection to the city of Smithfield, and now the Ava Gardner Museum, relocated to Market Street in the heart of downtown Smithfield, can tell you everything else you'd like to know about the beloved and much admired actress.

This Inmate Made Good Use of His Time!

The man everyone described as dapper and reserved with a slight Southern drawl had been convicted of embezzlement and sentenced to three years in an Ohio prison. He was the son of a North Carolina physician, lost his mother to tuberculosis, worked as a pharmacist, then worked on a ranch in Texas before becoming a bank teller. Convict Number 30664 seemed to carry with him an air of gentility that decried his tragic life and the crime of which he was convicted. Inmates and prison guards alike agreed: this well-spoken gentleman didn't belong behind prison walls and iron bars.

But the man served his time well and responsibly, and for the first time had a huge block of time in which to write. He took advantage of the three years, writing stories for magazines far from the Ohio prison walls. Most of his best friends and editorial associates in both North Carolina and New York were unaware of his incarceration or the conditions under which he was writing. It wasn't until his death that the truth finally came out: William Sydney Porter, who used the pen name O. Henry, had been imprisoned for three years for embezzling money from the First National Bank in Austin, Texas, where he had been a bank teller.

At the time of this charge, the young bank teller had jumped bond, supposedly heading to Honduras, which had no extradition treaty, but hastened back to Austin when he learned that his frail, sickly wife, Athol, was extremely ill. There he was tried for embezzlement and sent to the federal penitentiary in Columbus, Ohio.

Scholars and biographers still disagree as to whether or not he committed the crime, but in 1898 he began serving the sentence he referred to once as when he "fell heir to enough spare time to take up fiction writing seriously."

Some people shine under difficult circumstances. During his incarceration the author refined his writing and became known as the literary genius from whose pen flowed more than two hundred stories, including such classics as *The Gift of the Magi* and *The Ransom of Red Chief*.

You can see some artifacts relating to the life of William Sydney Porter at the Greensboro Historical Museum, and can visit his burial place at Riverside Cemetery in Asheville.

The Man Who Couldn't Go Home

He was a big man, well over six feet tall and with large feet. The man the world would come to know and celebrate as North Carolina's and perhaps America's most famous literary figure was born in Asheville. Thomas Wolfe was more at home in cities such as New York and Paris, far removed from the Blue Ridge Mountains that he said "imprisoned" his imagination. The words he wrote, "You can't go home again," apparently were true for him.

Some of his peers were put off by what they perceived as Wolfe's intellectual snobbery and egomania. At age sixteen, he once addressed the Dialectic Society of Chapel Hill assembled at the University of North Carolina and announced that one day his own portrait would hang right next to those of Confederate generals and ex-presidents (he was right).

He is best known for his novels *Look Homeward, Angel* and *Of Time and the River*. The former book—said to be the most autobiographical work of fiction by an American writer—so inflamed and insulted the people of Asheville that when Wolfe returned to the city of his birth, they threatened to tar and feather him.

He died in 1938 of tubercular meningitis, just shy of his thirty-eighth birthday. Wolfe is buried with other family members in Riverside Cemetery in Asheville. The boardinghouse called Old Kentucky Home, which his mother Julia owned and where he grew up, still stands (in *Angel,* Wolfe called the boardinghouse "Dixieland"). Although the house was damaged by fire in July 1998, you can tour the grounds and learn more of Wolfe's history from the docents.

It strikes many visitors as ironic that the home of the man who couldn't go home again is a popular tourist stop. Now known as the Thomas Wolfe Memorial, the home is frequented by fans and historians. Across the street and on a plaque by the curb of the Renaissance Hotel, you will find a pair of enormous shoes, a replica of the size thirteens worn by Wolfe. Bronzed by a local garden club, perhaps these wait for Wolfe to return, or for someone of his high literary caliber to come along and fill them one day.

N★C Stran©e . . . but true

The Story of Thomas Wolfe's Real Angel

When Thomas Wolfe was a young boy, his father, William Oliver Wolfe, had a tombstone shop at 28 Pack Square in Asheville. He once purchased an angel statue from Carrara, Italy—a marble piece with delicate details in which one hand held a lily, the other hand was raised in silent benediction, and one foot stood nearly on tiptoe. The angel sat on the front porch of W. O. Wolfe's shop for years, and later was the inspiration behind the title of Wolfe's first short story, "Angel on the Porch." Most people believe the title *Look Homeward, Angel* was also inspired by the statue, although those words were taken from Milton's classic poem "Lycidas."

The angel statue now stands sentinel in Oakdale Cemetery in Hendersonville, about twenty miles south of Asheville.

"Good Night, and Good Luck"

Born Egbert Roscoe Murrow in 1908 in Greensboro, he changed his first name to Edward. Hardworking and ambitious, Murrow put himself through college at Washington State while working in logging camps, then became assistant director of the Institute of International Education. This was a far cry from the profession he finally chose, and for which he is best remembered.

Murrow went to work for CBS in 1935, then became the director of the European Bureau in 1937. His descriptions of the Nazi takeover of Vienna enthralled his radio listeners, and in London when he sat on a rooftop to make his moment-by-moment description of German bombing raids he became as famous as any newscaster today. His signature saying as he was going off the air was, "Good night, and good luck."

Returning to New York, he coproduced a weekly radio program, but it was his television series, *See It Now*, that turned the tide of public sentiment against Senator Joseph McCarthy, known for his vehement and career-destroying accusations of Communist activity.

Cancer claimed the chain-smoking Murrow in 1965, but in his lifetime he helped set the standards for the journalistic profession.

For you, Mr. Murrow, "Good night, and good luck."

A World War II Vet Still in Great Shape!

Lying at anchor on the Cape Fear River in the City of Wilmington, the Battleship *North Carolina* still looks great and is an impressive sight up close. She's more than 728 feet long, with a beam of a little more than 108 feet, and has a displacement of 44,800 tons when fully loaded.

Commissioned in 1941, she was the first of ten battleships especially built for speed and power, a major naval force to be dealt with in World War II. The Battleship, well made for intensive confrontations, was a key player in every significant naval offensive in the Pacific Ocean, including Guadalcanal and Okinawa. She was outfitted with three turrets, each containing three 16-inch guns that could fire 2,700-pound shells up to 23 miles

The Battleship North Carolina *lies at anchor in Wilmington.* (COURTESY N.C. DIVISION OF TOURISM, FILM, AND SPORTS DEVELOPMENT)

away. She had enough additional firepower to bring 128 gun barrels to bear against any air target. With all this firepower in action, it often appeared from a distance that the ship was on fire.

In the Battleship's heyday, she was, for months on end, home to a crew of 2,339 men. The Battleship was its own self-contained city, with a bakery, hospital, movie theater, butcher shop, and general store. The crew slept stacked in bunk beds five-high, and feeding such a massive number of people was a challenge.

As an example, here's a list of ingredients for a pumpkin pie recipe served onboard (don't try this at home):

> 6 cases pumpkin
> 100 pounds sugar
> 30 gallons water
> 30 dozen eggs
> 22 pounds cornstarch

The Battleship earned fifteen battle stars for her distinguished service, which took her the equivalent of three times around the world. Those and her other war decorations are on her side, just like on a soldier's chest. The *North Carolina* was decommissioned in 1947 and made into a memorial in 1961, dedicated to the veterans of World War II from the Tarheel State.

Now you can tour the Battleship, walk the bridge, and see the kitchen, the gun turrets, the engine room, the pilot house, and more. Besides being impressed and stirred by the size of the ship and her history as you walk around the ship and grounds, you might see or hear more: some workers say the ship is haunted by the ghosts of five crewmen who were killed by an enemy torpedo during the war. The ghosts have even frequented places outside the ship, such as the gift shop.

One gift shop employee reports, "My coworker and I were getting ready to close up for the night. We were in the stockroom putting up merchandise when there was an extremely loud crash that sounded like glass breaking in the gift shop. We knew it had to be the glass cases shattering." Thinking it might be someone robbing the shop, the employees fled. Returning later with help, they found nothing out of place and everything intact. "All the cases were just the way we left them," the employee said. "But no one could tell us we hadn't heard what we heard. The sound of all those cases breaking was deafening."

When you visit, keep your eyes—and ears—open. Even in the gift shop.

It Started With a Mark on a Page

Governor Charles B. Aycock is known as North Carolina's "education governor." What is not so widely known is how and why he was so intent upon every person in the state being educated.

Born in Fremont in 1859 and the youngest of ten children, Charles was still a youngster when he witnessed something that altered his life. One day the county squire came by and needed Charles's mother's signature on a land deed. Instead of signing her name, his mother marked an X on the line where

Governor Charles B. Aycock took steps to ensure that every person in North Carolina could learn to read and write. (COURTESY N.C. DEPT. OF CULTURAL RESOURCES)

her signature would normally go. She admitted to a surprised Charles that she could neither read nor write. Even at his young age, Charles vowed to himself then and there that he would see to it that every man and woman in North Carolina would have the chance to read and write.

Because of the Civil War, Aycock was unable to begin school until he was eight years old. This delay did little to dissuade him. By age sixteen, Aycock was a teacher in a one-room schoolhouse. In 1877 he attended the

University of North Carolina and graduated in three years. In 1881 he was elected superintendent of public instruction for Wayne County, the only office he held other than governor.

Aycock developed oratory skills that lifted him in prominence with both parties. He galvanized both Democrats and Republicans into action, taking steps to ensure every person in North Carolina could learn to read and write. During his term from 1901 to 1905, a schoolhouse was built every day Aycock was governor—including Sundays.

After his term, he became a nationally recognized spokesperson for education, traveling from Maine to Oklahoma to share his vision of universal education. On April 4, 1912, during a speech in Birmingham, Alabama, he suffered a heart attack and died, with the word "education" the last word from his lips.

In 1932 in Statutory Hall in the U.S. Capitol, Aycock was honored by one of the two statues representing the best of North Carolina. On the hundredth anniversary of his birth, his birthplace in Fremont was made into a state historic site, one of the first in the state. The site has been restored to the way it appeared when it was a farmstead in the late 1860s and early 1870s, and includes a one-room schoolhouse, similar to the one in which Aycock taught. It is open every day except public holidays.

Often it's not the moments shared by thousands that affect millions—a small moment witnessed only by one or two people may change history. Such was the case of Charles Aycock and a mark on a page that changed the history of North Carolina and made him known forever as the "education governor."

A Mother Immortalized

Anna McNeill was born in Clarkton on a plantation called Oak Forest. At age twenty-seven she married a West Point graduate, and had five sons, one of whom moved to live in Paris. Anna then lost her husband and three sons to illness. When the Civil War broke out, Anna felt unsafe in the South because she had been married to a West Point man, so she joined her son in France.

There Anna became immortalized and her son famous. He was an artist and he had her sit for a portrait, entitling it *Arrangement in Grey and Black: The Artist's Mother.*

Had it not been for the Civil War and Anna McNeill Whistler's uneasiness at remaining in North Carolina, we might never have come to know her as *Whistler's Mother* and to know her son, James Whistler, and his resulting body of work.

Incidentally, the painting, owned by the government of France, is on exhibit at the Musée d'Orsay in Paris, and is a stunning work.

Guess Who?

This Winston-Salem native carved a niche for himself in sports journalism beginning in the 1950s. He often announced the matches of young boxer Cassius Clay, who changed his name to Muhammad Ali, and was a commentator for ABC's *Monday Night Football* in the 1970s. His name rapidly became well known because of his unapologetically acerbic interview style and critical diatribes.

Who was this announcer? The inimitable Howard Cosell, who was born Howard Cohen and changed his last name while in college.

Welcome to Mayberry

The streets of Mount Airy bring to mind the fictitious village of Mayberry from the long-running television show. Located just about seven miles south of the Virginia state line, the town is as colorful, warm, and quaint as your grandmother's handmade quilt.

It was here that Andy Griffith was born in 1935 to Carl and Geneva Griffith. A Depression-era baby, he learned the value of hard work and how to be resourceful with his talents. He had a quick wit, and many of his high school classmates at Rockford Street School referred to him as someone born to act.

Young Griffith also had musical talents; he learned to play the trombone from his minister, Reverend Ed Mickey, who presided over the Grace Moravian Church. The young man also took voice lessons and sang many solos at school and church events.

Griffith was possessed of a deep faith and pursued a degree in religion at the University of North Carolina at Chapel Hill. His acting talents would not be denied, however; he wound up as a member of the university theater group, The Playmakers, and changed his major to acting.

The rest is history: Andy Griffith got his first big break in Manteo, playing Sir Walter Raleigh in the play, *The Lost Colony*, about the missing colonists of Roanoke. From there he went to Broadway, starring in *No Time for Sergeants* and *Destry*. He made comedy records such as *What It Was, Was Football* and his own version of *Romeo and Juliet*. Most likely you know about his two blockbuster television series, *The Andy Griffith Show* and *Matlock*.

What you may not know is that through *The Andy Griffith Show*, one of television's most successful programs, the young man who veered away from a possible degree in divinity is today indirectly inspiring people to explore their faith and values.

In 1998, preacher Joey Fann, who presides over the Twickenham Church of Christ in Huntsville, Alabama, started a Bible study group that focuses on Mayberry episodes to teach examples of Christian struggles, hopes, and life lessons.

Dubbed "The Search for Mayberry," the lessons caught on with hundreds of church groups around the country. Complete with lesson plans and other guides, the themed Bible study is currently taught and used in about twenty churches in North Carolina, including the First Baptist Church in Albemarle, and Wrightsville United Methodist Church in Wrightsville Beach.

There doesn't seem to be a church conducting Mayberry-themed Bible studies in Mount Airy, but it's bound to happen.

Visiting Mayberry in Mount Airy

The Andy Griffith Show and the fictitious village of Mayberry continue to fascinate millions of Americans. In Mount Airy, Andy Griffith's former home at 711 Haymore Street has been turned into a bed and breakfast, where die-hard fans can spend the night in the rooms young Andy lived in. "We stay pretty much booked up," said Trudy Willard, the guest services manager. "It's been amazing how many people have come through town to stay here at Andy Griffith's boyhood home. When folks stay with us, we play music from the show and also let our guests view films from the series while they're here."

In addition, the city itself in some ways replicates the *Mayberry* set, complete with Floyd's Barber Shop. Mount Airy has capitalized on America's fascination with all things related to the series, and holds an annual *Andy Griffith Show*–themed festival called Mayberry Days. During the celebration, many of the show's characters make special appearances in town.

If you've been looking for Mayberry, now you know where to find it.

Helping Cure the Ills of Society

Near the middle of the nineteenth century a young girl named Elizabeth Blackwell decided she wanted to pursue a profession to which few women had aspired. She told her friend and minister-physician in Asheville, John Dickinson, that she would pay "whatever price demanded" to reach her goal of becoming a physician.

Blackwell was born in England and came to America with her parents when she was about ten years old. After her father's death, she and her two sisters started a private school in Cincinnati, Ohio. From there she taught in Kentucky, then found her way to North Carolina, where she took a teaching job in Asheville.

Blackwell, then twenty-five, realized that she had a penchant for curing the sick, and read everything she could about medicine. At this time she and Dickinson became friends, and he and his brother, a doctor in Charleston, South Carolina, loaned her medical reading materials.

When Blackwell announced her intention to obtain a medical license, Dickinson sent her to his brother, an instructor at Charleston Medical

College. There, Samuel Dickinson tutored her in the healing arts, for free.

Blackwell applied for admission to Harvard Medical School, then Yale, then Bowdoin. All rejected her. Other medical schools in New York City and Philadelphia were equally discouraging. Finally she was accepted to Geneva Medical School in New York, now a part of Syracuse University. She had applied at thirty institutions before being accepted.

Her college experience at Geneva was difficult. As the only female, many of her fellow students refused to acknowledge her presence, and some professors turned her away from

Elizabeth Blackwell was the first woman in the United States to receive a medical degree. (COURTESY N.C. DEPT. OF CULTURAL RESOURCES)

anatomy lessons. Despite this, Blackwell graduated in January 1849, with the highest honors of her class—becoming the first woman in the United States to receive a medical degree.

Blackwell's professional obstacles did not stop there. Turned away from clinics and hospitals, she went on to study obstetrics at a maternity hospital in Paris, then undertook further medical studies in London.

After returning to New York City, despite opposition and a lack of funds, Blackwell helped found the New York Infirmary for Women and Children in 1857 and the first Women's Medical College in 1868. Because of the opposition she faced, Blackwell became even more rigid in her resolve to further rights for women, and became known as "a militant suffragette."

Throughout the rest of her life, Elizabeth Blackwell was active in the struggle for women's rights. By means of her stubbornness, vision, and perseverance, she opened the way for women to enter the world of medicine.

N★C FAMOUS NORTH CAROLINIANS TRIVIA

Q. What broadcast journalist was born in Wilmington in 1920 and was teamed with co-anchor Chet Huntley on a news-and-commentary show?

A. David McClure Brinkley.

Q. What "poet of small-town America" who was also a newsman for CBS was born in Wilmington in 1934? (Hint: he is memorialized in a nature trail in Windsor, part of the Roanoke River National Wildlife Refuge.)

A. Charles Kurault, who looked for stories down the side roads and in small towns. His show was *On the Road with Charles Kurault*.

Q. What TV personality and comedian, whose real name is Milton Hines, was born in Franklinton?

A. Soupy Sales.

Q. What Emmy award–winning actress made her home in Siler City and played Aunt Bee on *The Andy Griffith Show*?

A. Frances Bavier. Her home still stands at 503 West Elk Street.

Q. In what North Carolina town did Marjorie Kinnan Rawlings write her novel *The Yearling*?

A. Banner Elk.

Q. What artist was fired from an Asheville construction company in 1924 for doodling on subdivision plats? (Hint: his first character was named Mickey.)

A. Walt Disney, who moved to California after he was fired. The plats are still on file in the Buncombe County Courthouse.

Q. What famous writer of the Jazz Age lived in the Grove Park Inn in Asheville in 1936?

A. F. Scott Fitzgerald.

Q. Who in 1953 was named North Carolina's first poet laureate?

A. James Larkin Pearson.

Q. What Chatham County slave wrote *The Hope of Liberty*, which was the first book by a black author in the South?

A. George Moses Horton.

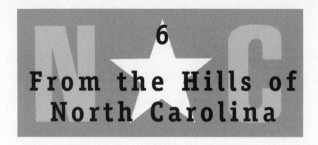

6
From the Hills of North Carolina

Oh, to What Heights They Will Go!

The Smoky Mountains' highest mountain is named in honor of the late professor Elisha Mitchell, with an unusual story behind the naming of Mount Mitchell.

It started with a dispute between mountain explorer and Tennessee senator Thomas Lanier Clingman and Mitchell, a professor at the University of North Carolina, about what peak in the Appalachian Mountains was the highest. Mitchell claimed Black Dome in North Carolina; Clingman said Tennessee's Smoky Dome had that honor.

While doing altitude checks of Black Dome, Mitchell drowned in a stream. After this, Clingman hired Arnold Guyot, a Swiss-born geographer, to make a study of the mountains. At 6,643 feet, Smoky Dome (now Clingman's Dome) is the highest point in Tennessee—but Black Dome (now Mount Mitchell) won the contest, at 6,684 feet.

Today you can visit the Mount Mitchell State Park and Museum, which offers many ways to learn more about the mountain that caused such a stir.

This Should "Peak" Your Interest

The only county in the entire United States with a mountain range lying completely within its borders is the Piedmont's Stokes County. The mountain range is Sauratown Range, an ancient range named for the Saura Indians.

The Vanderbilt Legacy in North Carolina

At the time of his father's death in 1885, George Washington Vanderbilt was considered the world's most eligible and wealthy bachelor. The twenty-three-year-old heir to part of his father's $200 million estate, this youngest son had been raised in New York City and was both well educated (with a reading knowledge of eight languages besides English) and well traveled. But in 1888 he was bitten by the love bug.

This young heir was smitten not with a woman, but with a place. When he visited the mountainous and breathtaking area of Asheville, Vanderbilt knew he had to make his home in the area.

The Biltmore House in Asheville is the largest privately owned home in the world. (PHOTO BY JAMES VALENTINE, © BILTMORE COMPANY. USED WITH PERMISSION)

He initially thought to build a "modest winter retreat" to escape the inclement and cold weather in New York. To carry out his vision, Vanderbilt appointed experienced craftsmen especially trained in the ways of the Old World. For home design, he chose architect Richard Morris Hunt, and for the landscaping and grounds design, Frederick Law Olmsted, who designed New York City's Central Park. For this winter home he chose a lovely wooded area outside Asheville.

As time passed, architect Hunt's plans evolved and grew to resemble a European castle more than an Appalachian mountain retreat. Vanderbilt's acreage also increased as he continued to expand his landholdings, eventually reaching 125,000 acres, including Mount Pisgah.

As any homebuilder can tell you, construction always costs more and takes longer than you anticipate. Vanderbilt's house project took six years to complete, but what we know today as Biltmore House is unlike anything else in America.

From banquet hall to library (with walls of leather-bound volumes) to swimming pool to its thirty-four bedrooms, Biltmore House impresses all who see it. It is now open to the public, preserved by Vanderbilt descendants. Biltmore Estate itself includes the house, a winery, vineyards, lovely gardens, and an inn with more than two hundred rooms.

Biltmore House is listed in the *Guinness Book of World Records* as the largest privately owned home in the world. While much of the other Vanderbilts' fortunes have been spent on things long forgotten, George Vanderbilt created an enduring masterpiece with Old World elegance that continues to delight and awe people.

Did You Know? The first part of the name Biltmore was taken from the word "Bildt," the name of the Dutch town of George Vanderbilt's ancestors. The "more" part is an old English word meaning "open, rolling land."

A Tragic Page in History

On April 7, 1838, General Winfield Scott sent his superiors this message: "I shall probably call for the following detachments of militia to rendezvous at the places mentioned, two regiments of 1,840 Georgians to rendezvous at New Echota, one regiment of 750 Alabamians to rendezvous at Belfont, one regiment of 740 North Carolinians to rendezvous at Franklin, NC, one regiment of 740 Tennesseans to rendezvous at Ross Landing. 3,700 troops plus 2,200 regulars. Subsistence for the foregoing troops at the places mentioned will be required for 90 days, commencing about the middle of May."

Scott wasn't gathering the regiments for battle, but to round up Native American people living in and near there, for the long, bitter march we now know as the Trail of Tears. More than four thousand Native American men, women and children perished in 1838 as a result.

The Rebirth of a Nation

The Eastern Band of the Cherokee Nation has a long and proud history of not only surviving but thriving despite circumstances that would have wiped out lesser people. Known as one of the "Five Civilized Tribes," before encroachment of white settlers, the Cherokee had a constitution; a capitol in New Echota, Georgia; their own written language; and their own newspaper, the *Cherokee Phoenix*.

You might think that these attributes would have encouraged white settlers to live peacefully with the Cherokee, but this was not the case. Whites seemed even more determined to take over the Cherokee tribal lands.

In 1835 tribal leaders saw resistance was futile, so they signed the Treaty of New Echota, which stated they would move to seven million acres "in the Arkansas River region" as their new homeland. In turn, the U.S. government under President Andrew Jackson agreed to set aside two thousand dollars annually to educate Cherokee children and provide the departing families with various equipment and supplies. It also agreed to replace the printing press and type that white people had recently destroyed.

Scouts began rounding up Cherokee people. Approximately a thousand hid out in the mountains under the leadership of Utsali, also known as Lichen. One Cherokee man, Tsali, was in his cabin with his wife and children when scouts arrived and ordered them to pack what they could carry and walk to the stockade in Bushnell (now under the waters of Fontana Lake). They were joined by Tsali's brother-in-law and proceeded to the stockade under guard.

The march west, known today as the Trail of Tears, began in 1838 from Bushnell, led by General Winfield Scott. Along the trail, many of the Cherokee began dying. The old people and the very young were the most vulnerable to illness and death, as the uniformed soldiers prodded them along—sometimes with bayonets.

When Tsali's wife, Wilani, stumbled and fell, she was prodded with a soldier's bayonet. Tsali held his anger and decided on a course of action. He told his relatives in Cherokee that at the next bend in the trail, he would trip and fall, saying he had injured his ankle. By creating a distraction, Tsali and his family escaped the soldiers, but during the struggle one soldier was killed. Suddenly Tsali and his family were not only fugitives, but wanted for murder. The family took refuge in a cave under Clingman's Dome. Meanwhile, Utsali's band of Cherokee continued to elude capture in the mountains.

Through a trader, Scott offered to let Utsali's band stay in the mountains if Tsali, his brother-in-law, and sons surrendered. Tsali agreed.

Although his youngest son (Wasituna, called Washington by white people) and Wilani were spared, Tsali (his brother-in-law) and two of his sons were taken to be executed. Tsali's last request was that he be shot, not by white soldiers, but by his own people. Three Cherokee men were chosen to be the executioners.

Because of Tsali's sacrifice, the Cherokee who remained in the mountains began to thrive. The descendants of those who escaped the Trail of Tears now live on the Cherokee Reservation known as the Qualla Boundary, near western North Carolina.

The Trail of Tears and Tsali's sacrifice are remembered in the drama Unto These Hills, *performed at Qualla Boundary*. (COURTESY CHEROKEE HISTORICAL ASSOCIATION)

Today, the reservation is a thriving community and popular tourist stop, with various attractions. The play, *Unto These Hills,* depicts the history of the Cherokee and Tsali's sacrifice, and more than one hundred thousand people saw it during its opening season in 1950. Also within the reservation is the Oconaluftee Indian Village, a unique re-creation of a Cherokee community in the eighteenth century. This was created in 1952 by a cooperative effort of anthropological experts from the University of Georgia, University of Tennessee, and University of North Carolina, under the supervision of the reservation-based Tsali Institute for Cherokee Indian Research.

Also within the reservation is the Museum of the Cherokee Indian, one of the oldest Indian museums in the United States, with state-of-the-art exhibits. The museum also publishes the *Journal of Cherokee Studies*, the oldest journal devoted specifically to one tribal group.

Today the reservation of fifty-six thousand acres is visited by more than a million people a year. Located at the North Carolina entrance to the Great Smoky Mountains National Park and at the terminus of the Blue Ridge Parkway, the Qualla Boundary offers easy access to visitors from those destinations. Today you can visit and learn more about a people who might have been lost were it not for the sacrifice of Tsali and his family.

A Moonshine Story

The Appalachian Mountains of western North Carolina have historically been home to people who made illegal whiskey, called moonshine. It might be illegal, but to those in the mountains, it was tradition.

The making of moonshine has long been a cherished family tradition among the people of this area, dating to the post–Revolutionary War years. In appreciation for their contribution, veterans of this war were given certificates exempting them from the law that made it illegal to make and sell whiskey. They took advantage of this and industriously created their own versions of various homemade spirits. The next generation followed suit, as did the next. The practice became a family tradition, with descendants of the original moonshiners believing that the exemptions their fathers had enjoyed were "passed down" to them. Being upstanding, God-fearing citizens didn't interfere with making moonshine, which they considered their right. Although the numbers of moonshiners have dwindled, they still exist.

In January 1951 a magazine called the *State* reported that in one county alone, 264 stills were seized and fourteen operators arrested the previous year. If you want to see a still up close, one captured by agents in the 1960s is on display in the Appalachian Cultural Museum, which is part of Appalachian State University in Boone.

Did You Know? The term *moonshiner* came about because the illegal whiskey-making business was safest at night. Those who sold the contraband were called bootleggers because they often hid bottles of whiskey in the top of their loose-fitting boots. What started as moonshine running (or whiskey tripping) in automobiles racing to escape "revenuers" became the billion-dollar industry known as stock car racing.

Did You Know? The oldest frame house west of the Blue Ridge Mountains is the Allison-Deaver Home in Brevard, dating back to 1815. Open to the public, the house is unique because nothing has been changed in any way—the wall paneling and paint, the structure, and the interior furnishings remain as they were. The only work done on the house has been when repairs were necessary for restoration.

The Mystery of Eric Rudolph's Fate

In January 1998 a bomb exploded outside a women's health clinic called the New Woman in Birmingham, Alabama. Eric Robert Rudolph was seen running from the clinic wearing a wig and jumping into his pickup truck immediately after the explosion. This was the first fatal bombing of an abortion clinic, killing a police officer and critically wounding a nurse.

Initially the FBI thought it was seeking Tarheel native Rudolph as a witness, but by February his status was changed to "main suspect." His story and likeness aired nationally on the TV show *America's Most Wanted*. The FBI also garnered the help of hundreds of volunteers to search for him, and offered a $1 million reward for information leading to his arrest.

Rudolph had fled to somewhere in the mountains of southwestern North Carolina. As time went on and the investigation into the Alabama bombing continued, clues were unearthed linking that bombing to three bomb attacks in Atlanta—one at the 1996 Olympic Games. This prompted the FBI to add Rudolph to its Most Wanted List.

Many highly trained agents looked for the fugitive, but Rudolph had the home advantage. He had grown up in the rugged backcountry near Murphy, and was skilled in outdoor survival. In July, Rudolph was seen in the town of Andrews, where he reportedly stole a pickup truck and food from a residence near the 530,000-acre Nantahala National Forest. As months passed, agents would come close to finding Rudolph, but he was always just one step ahead. The forest where he reportedly sought refuge was one he had often explored as a child.

The ever-present FBI agents in the previously serene town of Andrews created a division in the community. Some residents thought of Rudolph as an outlaw, while others viewed him as a bringer of justice and protector of the unborn.

Although some locals helped the FBI find caves or old mines in the area that might serve as hiding places, the elusive Rudolph did not turn up. An entourage of volunteer former Green Berets searched, to no avail. As the search dragged on, local businesses began to benefit from extra income as a result of the media exposure and increased traffic, and even posted humorous signs outside their establishments to encourage people to stop in. The Lake's End Grill, for example, had on their marquee, "Rudolph Eats Here."

In November 15, 2000, with a cold trail and no suspect in custody, grand juries in Atlanta, Georgia, and Birmingham, Alabama, indicted Eric Robert Rudolph on twenty-three counts for the violent acts. He remains on the FBI's Most Wanted List. Most of the experts connected with the manhunt insist that Rudolph is dead, although others say he is somewhere on the Appalachian Trail.

A reward of $1 million for Eric Rudolph still stands.

An Odd Population

In Flat Rock you'll find the former home of famous author Carl Sandburg—poet, "champion of the common man," and biographer of Abraham Lincoln. His home, now maintained as a National Historic Site by the U.S. Park Service, was named Connemara by the original owner, who was Irish. Today the grounds of Connemara are inhabited by goats. Sandburg's wife, Lillian, had as many as two hundred Chickaming goats on the grounds of Connemara at one time. Their goats now graze—or "grace"—the property.

N★C HILLS OF NORTH CAROLINA TRIVIA

Q. What county is known as the Heart of the Blue Ridge?

A. Yancey.

Q. What county calls itself the Jewel of the Blue Ridge?

A. Madison County, because it offers diverse outdoor activities, scenic beauty—and the only hot mineral spring in the state.

Q. What county calls itself the Land of Waterfalls?

A. Transylvania, with more than 250 waterfalls within its borders.

Q. Approximately how many visitors come to see the Biltmore House annually?

A. 700,000.

Q. What is the name of the largest recreation area on the Blue Ridge Parkway?

A. Doughton Park.

Q. What town is known as Sourwood City because of its many sourwood trees (which produce a delicious honey as well)?

A. Black Mountain.

Q. Where can you find the annual Gee-Haw Whimmy Diddle (a toy unique to Appalachia) Competition?

A. Southern Highland Handicraft Guild Folk Art Center, just outside Asheville.

Q. Where was the site of the first execution (and only hanging) of a woman in North Carolina?

A. Morganton, which was where convicted murderess Frankie Silver was hung in 1832.

Q. What was the first ski resort in the South?

A. Cataloochee Ski Area, in Maggie Valley.

7
Religion and Unique Communities

Cursed by a Man of the Cloth

In 1705 Bath was the first settlement the North Carolina Assembly incorporated as a town. By the early eighteenth century Bath was a thriving seaport (and home to a few pirates—but that's in another chapter) on the shoreline of North Carolina and at the mouth of the Pamlico River. However, one evangelist is said to have changed the luck of the town.

Evangelist George Whitefield came to Bath around 1747. He began exhorting the people against what he called deadly sins—cursing, drinking, and dancing. He was most adamantly against the latter.

This traveling preacher apparently was always prepared for his own trip to Heaven, because oddly enough, he carried his coffin in his wagon wherever he went. "When I pass on," he reportedly said, "I want my coffin right here." Even more bizarre was his habit of sleeping in his coffin at night, supposedly to avoid the inn and its attendant shady goings-on.

Whitefield finally gave up on converting Bath and the people who looked at him with more than a little suspicion. Just like the disciples of old, he drove his wagon to the outskirts of town, removed his shoes, shook the dirt from them, and put a curse on the town. He told onlookers that the Bible said people who couldn't get sinners to reform were to do just what he had done, and by shaking the dust of Bath from his shoes, the town would be cursed for its hardness of heart against the Word.

He is quoted as having said, "I say to the village of Bath, village you shall remain, now and forever, forgotten by men and nations until such time as it pleases God to turn the light of His countenance again upon you."

Since Whitefield's curse, downtown Bath has been struck three times by fire, and it remains a sleepy (but charming) little village on the coast.

Stories of Snake Handlers

Differences in interpreting the Holy Scriptures have often led to new and sometimes unusual religions and cults. One of these religions involves serpent handling, founded on the Gospel of Saint Mark (16:18): "And they shall take up serpents. . . " The Gospel of Mark also referred to spirit-filled people having the ability to speak in tongues and drink "any deadly thing" without injury.

Many people who participate in speaking in tongues and drinking deadly substances (including strychnine and lye) consider themselves to be simply following the word of God, and not doing anything unusual. If they get bitten or die, then it is God's will that it is their time and has nothing to do with their lack of faith or God's protection.

George Went Hensley is generally given credit for introducing handling of serpents as a religious rite. It began in Ooltewah, Tennessee, at Rainbow Rock on White Oak Mountain around 1905 (although some accounts place the first handling around 1908). Hensley had led a tumultuous life, but was converted and began to follow all the teachings of God, including what he believed the Gospel of Mark dictated: that the truly faithful should handle serpents and drink toxic substances as part of their religious practices.

Many churches took up the practice back then, and it was most popular in Tennessee, West Virginia, Kentucky, and North Carolina. While believers saw snake handling as following the word of God, the rest of society considered it bizarre and abnormal. Finally, in the 1940s state legislatures began to make snake handling illegal, and North Carolina outlawed it in 1949. Despite this legislation, many refused to cease handling snakes, saying they were following God's law. Many died from being bitten—including Hensley in 1955, after handling his last rattlesnake.

The House of Prayer in the Name of Jesus Christ in Marshall still practices snake handling, and is the only place of worship in the Tarheel State that clings to this literal interpretation of the writings of Mark. Charles Prince, one of the more well-known proponents of snake handling in North Carolina, died of a rattlesnake bite in 1985, just as Hensley had.

The preacher at the House of Prayer won't give interviews, and if you go to a service there, no one can guarantee you'll see snake handling. Believers say that particular activity is a spontaneous, spirit-led phenomenon—and not something one can schedule into a service.

Preacher Charles Prince was arrested for handling deadly snakes during an outdoor worship service held behind his bait shop in Canton. (One of the arresting officers was bitten by a yellow timber rattlesnake and required hospitalization.) (PHOTO © MIKE DUBOSE)

N★C Str/an@e . . . but true

The Church Moved by Divine Forces

In the late 1800s, many churches were built in Hyde County. The town of Swan Quarter has a church whose very foundations were, so the story goes, laid by divine hands.

In 1876 some Methodists in town wanted to build a new church, and found the perfect site. The owner, however, said the land was not for sale, and wouldn't budge no matter how the Methodists pleaded their cause.

So they built their little house of worship, called Providence Church, on another site not far from where they believed God really wanted it. Not long after this, a fierce hurricane swept through Swan Quarter. During the tempest, the church building was lifted from its foundation, and floated down the street on the resulting tidal surge. It came to rest—where else?—on the very land where the Methodist flock said it should have been all along.

The landowner saw the wisdom in leaving the church where the hurricane had placed it, and since then, Providence Church is known as the Church Moved by the Hand of God.

The Religion of the Lost Cause

Before the Civil War, preachers shouted sermons from pulpits in support of the South. When war broke out, those preachers fervently rallied their flocks to stay true to the South's cause. They claimed that every Confederate victory was a sign of God's love for the new nation, every defeat an indication of God's wrath.

After the Civil War, those religious leaders strove to help people make sense out of their defeat, and created a religion: the Religion of the Lost Cause. After all, Southerners observed, we can only become perfect through suffering.

Every faith has its martyrs and the Confederate States of America had many, from its generals to its president to its fallen sons and daughters. Robert E. Lee, Stonewall Jackson, and Jefferson Davis became mythic figures—to some, almost saint-like.

Terry Matthews, Ph.D., of Wake Forest University has lectured on this religious phenomenon in his course, Religion in the South. He describes this post-war religion as a "mixture of Southern nationalism and evangelicalism" aimed at recreating a perceived "golden age." Many Southerners saw some instances in Lee's life, he says, as parallel to the life of Jesus Christ. For example, Lee's decision to reject command of the Union Army was seen by followers as "the equal of Christ's temptation in the wilderness" and fighting the Union Army was an example of Good fighting Evil. In the new religion, the North was an evil "marauding monster," and the South everything that was pure and godly.

In his lecture, "Baptized in Blood: The Religion of the Lost Cause," Matthews says this new religion helped further the dream of "a cohesive South with a separate cultural identity," which became even more important after the war. This fervor with which followers embraced the notion of keeping the South "pure" later contributed to rampant lynchings.

In keeping with this new faith, Southerners boycotted national holidays such as Thanksgiving and the Fourth of July, but Lee's birthday of January 19 became a holiday throughout the South. Among the many Civil War memorials and statuary the South erected during 1890 to 1910, you will find one at Duke Chapel in Durham: a statue of Lee, standing right there with the saints.

General Robert E. Lee became the Christ figure of the Religion of the Lost Cause. (NATIONAL ARCHIVES)

The Enduring Mystery and Legacy of Roanoke

In the 1580s, England decided to send a fleet of ships and colonists to the New World, where Spain and France had failed at colonization. What piqued the interest of Queen Elizabeth I (daughter of Henry VIII) were rumors of Spanish galleons returning to their home ports laden with treasures of precious metals and lumber from the New World. While Spain retained claim to the newly discovered continent, England decided that a colony far enough away from Spanish efforts might just work, and Elizabeth sent Sir Humphrey Gilbert, who returned home after a brief stay in Newfoundland.

The next person chosen to carry out the charter was Gilbert's cousin, Sir Walter Raleigh, who had a burning desire to show England the feasibility of a colony in the New World. Raleigh worked quickly to gather a crew to send on the venture.

On July 4, 1584, the crew sighted land—the shoreline of what is now North Carolina—and gathered specimens of plant and animal life and drew maps of the area. They took these back home, along with two Native Americans, Manteo and Wanchese, as specimens of humanity that existed there. Raleigh's marketing tactics were on target: the English people were enthralled by the sight of the two aboriginal men and the amazing stories of the New World. Raleigh received more money to supply and fund the next voyage and additional ships.

After one bungled attempt at a settlement (they arrived too late to plant crops to tide them over the winter) in May 1585, Governor John White arrived in Roanoke with 113 men, women, and children. They repaired the cottages left by the first settlers and built new ones. On August 18 the first English child born in the New World was delivered. Her name was Virginia Dare.

Like the previous settlers' attempt, these people had also arrived too late for crops to sustain them through the winter. Governor White returned to England to expedite shipments to help his colony survive the winter.

When he arrived in England, however, no ships could be spared; England was about to defend herself against Spain. White would not return to Roanoke Island until three years later, in 1590. When he did, he found the colony deserted, with deer and other wildlife roaming the houses and weeds growing in abundance. The only clues about what had happened to the New World's first colonists were carvings on a tree and a post: CROATOAN and CRO. The colonists were never seen again, and White eventually returned to England.

What happened to the people of what is now called the Lost Colony? No one will ever know for certain, although quite a few have ventured hypotheses. Many historians believe that the carvings indicated the colonists had moved to Croatoan Island, fifty miles away, now the southern part of Hatteras Island. This theory is borne out by a report that in 1701, surveyor John Lawson traveled to Croatoan Island and met gray-eyed Hatteras Indians who were familiar with books and indicated that their ancestors were white people. If this theory is correct, then the

Did You Know? One of the Native Americans Sir Walter Raleigh brought to London was named Manteo. North Carolina eventually named a coastal town after this man, and it is here, in the city of Manteo, that every year the drama of the Lost Colony is played out on stage throughout the summer months.

The Roanoke mystery is dramatized in The Lost Colony, *performed in Manteo.*
(COURTESY N.C. DIVISION OF TOURISM, FILM, AND SPORTS DEVELOPMENT)

settlers of the "Lost Colony" were never lost, just absorbed by their environment and their new friends. Findings from archaeological digs, including copper farthings, lead shot, and gun flints, seem to support this conclusion.

Regardless, historians believe that the Roanoke colony was a success. The information from the initial explorers on Roanoke's first sailing proved invaluable toward establishing a successful colony further north.

That colony was Jamestown, Virginia, settled in 1607. While Raleigh's dream of establishing the first permanent colony in America was not realized, he did manage to fuel the imaginations of English people everywhere.

The Serendipitous Utopia

While most, if not all, utopian colonies and societies are planned, this one happened in a rather serendipitous fashion. Even odder is the fact that it came about because of World War I.

Once war was announced in April 1917, the enemy's commercial ships were seized in American ports. One of the ships seized on April 6, 1917, was the largest ship in the world, the *Vaterland*. The seized *Vaterland* and other German and Austrian vessels were overhauled and converted to U.S. troopships, and the U.S. government set about trying to find a place to keep the sailors from these ships, referred to as "enemy aliens."

In looking for a temporary home for the detainees, the government search team discovered the small, quiet town of Hot Springs, North Carolina. The town had a beautifully appointed and large inn called the Mountain Park Hotel. On two hundred acres of rolling lands, it was a resort famous for the health-giving hot bubbling springs the town was named for. Once the hotel owner agreed to the terms set by the government (a monthly payment among other things), the guests were asked to leave and preparations began for the arrival of the more than two thousand Germans, mostly civilians. New structures such as a barracks, water tower, mess hall, and guardhouses were built, as well as everything else this strange "city" would need, including a hospital (which was transformed from Hampton College). An eight-foot board fence topped with barbed wire was installed around the

2,251-foot perimeter of the former resort. Seven acres of the hotel grounds were made into a garden to raise food.

It is difficult to imagine the reaction of the 650 inhabitants of that small village on June 8, 1917, when the first eighteen unwilling guests the locals called "Germanies" arrived. The population of the camp continued to swell until by 1918 it had reached 2,185 men—more than triple the town's inhabitants.

Nearly thirty of the sailors' wives and children also arrived and boarded with Hot Springs families so they could be near their husbands and fathers. After a time, the townspeople realized that there were talents and skills to be shared with and learned from their new neighbors. German was spoken on the streets, the children attended school together, German housewives taught some of the local women fine needle working, and "alien" wives were regularly invited to tea with their American neighbors. The German internees showed their industriousness by using their skills in the garden, in raising animals, or in shoe cobbling or cooking. Guards and their captors formed friendships, and guards began taking new friends home for dinner. With the internment of the thirty-five-member German Imperial Band, many a Sunday afternoon found the locals enjoying the band's performances, described by one news reporter as every bit as good as the Boston Symphony Orchestra. The teachers at nearby Dorland Institute arranged for some of the camp members to come give talks to their students, in a cultural exchange of sorts. The prison had become a type of paradise, it seems, for only one German ever tried to escape—he was, in fact, successful and never seen or heard from again.

The interned men created their own German village with cottages, fences, and even a chapel, all in the Old World style. Some of the buildings became artists' studios and woodworking shops. Newspapers from New York to San Francisco carried stories of the internment camp; the *New York Times* expressed the hope that American prisoners of war would be treated just as well.

But this utopia was not to endure. In July 1918 the Department of Labor and the secretary of state made a joint decision to concentrate all prisoners of war, both civilian and soldier, at the War Prison Barracks in Fort

Oglethorpe, Georgia. The Hot Springs "aristocrats," as the *Asheville Citizen* called them, would have to live the life of other prisoners of war.

On the day the men were to leave, some speculate that, in an attempt to stay, they deliberately poisoned their drinking water. Whatever the cause, by the end of the day on August 1, 1918, more than 110 cases of typhoid fever had gripped the camp. Seventeen of the men died at Hot Springs, eighteen others died at a hospital in Asheville, and twenty-six stayed behind until they were fit for travel. On August 31 the remaining men were taken to Fort Oglethorpe, and by the end of September, the formerly bustling town of nearly 3,400 had shrunk to its original 650 residents.

Shortly after Armistice Day in November 1918, the charming, painstakingly erected buildings of the compound were blown up, one by one, by the townspeople. The Mountain Park Hotel and last remaining vestiges of the camp burned in 1920. The "accidental utopia" was no more; all that remains are the steps of the old inn.

In 1932 the American Legion of Asheville held a dedication ceremony on the camp site. It was attended by German dignitaries and by nearly four thousand spectators and aired both in the United States and over German airwaves.

Although unplanned and unforeseen, the Hot Springs internment camp led to understanding between some of the two countries' people. Author Jacqueline Burin Painter wrote in *The German Invasion of Western North Carolina* (Asheville: Biltmore Press, 1992) that this camp was "an example for the world . . . truly one of western North Carolina's finest hours."

Bethabara: The Moravian Settlement

The Moravian Church is a Protestant denomination with roots in Hernhut, Saxony, in the early eighteenth century. In 1753 the site was chosen for what would become the first Moravian settlement in North Carolina. Named Bethabara, which translates to "house of passage," it was meant to be a temporary settlement until the town of Salem could be completed.

Bethabara flourished and until 1772 served as the area's trade and religious center.

Near Bethabara, some Moravian Germans settled in Salem. Salem later merged with Winston, becoming Winston-Salem. Now both Bethabara and Winston-Salem are popular with visitors who love history, shopping, and stepping back in time. The area remains one of the most authentic and documented colonial sites in the United States, and Bethabara itself is a National Historic Landmark.

Also called the Unitas Fratrum, or the American branch of the Renewed Church of the Unity of Brethren, the Moravian Church is separated into north and south provinces. The Northern Province has its U.S. head-

Costumed guides give tours of the restored 1788 Gemeinhaus (German for "people's church") in Historic Bethabara Park, the site of the first Moravian settlement in North Carolina. (COURTESY N.C. DIVISION OF TOURISM, FILM, AND SPORTS DEVELOPMENT)

quarters in Bethlehem, Pennsylvania; the Southern Province, in Winston-Salem. Moravians emphasize fellowship and missionary work, and their church music (especially their singing) is known around the world.

Did You Know? The tiny town of Bolivia has a Buddhist temple. Dedicated to the much-beloved and venerated king of Thailand, the Wat Carolina Buddhajakra Vanaram (wat is Thai for "temple") houses monks who represent an unbroken lineage of twenty-five hundred years.

The Dam That Built a Town

The year was 1941, just a few weeks after the disaster at Pearl Harbor. To fuel the United States' efforts in World War II, hydroelectric power was needed. Government officials from the Tennessee Valley Authority picked a spot to establish a dam that would provide such power, in an isolated area between Joyce Kilmer Memorial Forest and the Great Smoky Mountains National Park. Within a few more weeks, more than six thousand workers arrived to build the dam, accompanied by their families.

The workers and their families needed accommodations and in short order cottages, a school, a church, and a hospital were built. For years the incidental community was home, supplying the workers and their families with a social life, an education, and a sense of history. In 1945, with the dam completed, the workers were no longer needed and they scattered, abandoning the place known as Fontana Village.

Today, Fontana Dam is open for tours, with a tram to take visitors to the

There was always time for family fun at Fontana Village. (COURTESY FONTANA VILLAGE)

bottom. The top of the dam is accessible by foot and is where the Appalachian Trail continues.

And what of the small community that was once home to the dam builders and their families? Fontana Village was turned into a vacation spot after the war, and the cottages originally built as part of the war effort are now available for families coming to visit the area.

One interesting footnote is the club called the Dam Kids, made up of workers' children who lived at Fontana Village during the years the dam was constructed. Every year, the Dam Kids hold their annual reunion at Fontana Village, the place they all once called home.

Did You Know? America's smallest town lies within the borders of North Carolina. With the latest census showing a population of only eleven people, Dellview in Gaston County wins the honor, hands down—a very few hands down.

Ethics: Alive and Well in the Tarheel State

Founded in 1987, the North Carolina Society for Ethical Culture meets every Sunday at the Community Arts Center in the town of Carrboro. Headquartered in Chapel Hill, this is one of twenty-two societies in the United States that make up the American Ethical Union. Ethical Culture was founded by social reformer Felix Adler in 1876 as a movement toward humanistic, educational, and religious concepts. Members are committed to ideals such as the worth of the human individual, improving relation-ships, and bringing out the best in oneself and others.

Like any other church gathering, this forty-five-plus member group also regularly gathers for potlucks. If you're in Carrboro around midday any Sunday, sit in on a meeting and become enlightened—and maybe fed, too.

Plaid to the Bone

Many colonists came to America in search of religious and political freedom, and many descendants of the Highland Scots live along the coast in the Tarheel State. The Highlands of Scotland is a mountainous region that was led by lords who ruled their own clans. Many fled from there to America, specifically North Carolina, to escape persecution after their involvement in the Jacobite uprisings of 1715 and 1745. During these conflicts they attempted to place the heirs of James II on the throne of England.

Today, there is a huge community of the descendants of "Scotland's greatest export." They reside in the Cape Fear River region and have greatly influenced the progress of the area. In the town of Red Springs, they founded a women's college in 1896. Named after Flora Macdonald, a Scottish heroine and political activitist who briefly made her home in the area (between 1774 and 1780), it was the only women's college in southeastern North Carolina until the middle of the twentieth century. Although Flora Macdonald College closed its doors in 1961, the campus of Flora Macdonald Academy (it has been renamed and is now a private

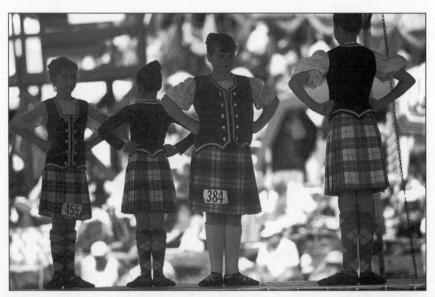

The annual Highland Games held at Grandfather Mountain celebrate the area's Scottish heritage. (COURTESY N.C. DIVISION OF TOURISM, FILM, AND SPORTS DEVELOPMENT)

school for pre-kindergarten through twelfth grade) is a National Historic Site. Ten acres adjacent to the academy have been turned into a lovely garden also named after Macdonald. Both the academy and the gardens are open to the public.

Red Springs is also the home of the Flora Macdonald Highland Games, in which the people celebrate their Scottish heritage with music, dancing, kilt wearing, and various competitions. To complement this festival, the Highland Games and Gathering of Scottish Clans is held in mid-July every year at Grandfather Mountain.

N★C RELIGION AND UNIQUE COMMUNITIES TRIVIA

Q. What man is referred to as the "Pope of Protestant America" for his far-reaching ability to evangelize to people all over the world?

A. Charlotte-born William Franklin Graham Jr.—known as Reverend Billy Graham.

Q. What museum in Lake Junaluska features the largest U.S. collection of artifacts pertaining to John Wesley and other Methodist church founders?

A. The World Methodist Museum.

Q. What religious group, dating to the Middle Ages, settled the town of Valdese?

A. The Waldensians.

Q. What city in North Carolina once was nicknamed the City of Temples?

A. Asheville.

Q. Where does the Southern Baptist Convention hold its conferences in North Carolina?

A. Ridgecrest.

Q. In the early eighteenth century, what religious group settled the town of Belvidere?

A. The Quakers.

Q. The Southeastern Baptist Theological Seminary makes its home in what town?

A. Wake Forest.

Q. What colony with an Alpine flavor did Heriot Clarkson found in 1910?

A. Little Switzerland.

Q. What Amish-Mennonite community existed only from 1907 to 1935 in the northeast corner of the state?

A. Pudding Ridge.

Q. What was the name of the Methodist preacher who rode circuit around the 1780s and named the town of Sligo after his birthplace in Ireland?

A. Reverend Edward Drumgoogle.

You Never Forget Your First Home Run

It was 1914 and the young man named George had arrived with his Baltimore Oriole teammates for three weeks of spring training in Fayetteville. It must have been a big year for the eighteen-year-old, staying for perhaps his first time at a hotel (Lafayette Hotel) with his teammates, away from St. Mary's boarding school where he had been raised.

Playing an intra-squad game at the former Cape Fear Fairgrounds near Gillespie Street, the rookie player came up to bat. As batboy Maurice Fleishman watched, bat connected with ball in the "c-r-a-c-k" sound every ball player and fan loves to hear, then the ball arched up, up, and away, for a total of 405 feet. Out of the park it went, over a nearby cornfield it flew, then it plopped into a lake, as young George enjoyed his first home run as a professional baseball player.

Then a smile lit up his cherubic face, which was so youthful that the other team members had nicknamed him "Babe." This was George Herman Ruth Jr.—the man the world remembers as Babe Ruth.

The Babe went on to enjoy an illustrious career, first with the Orioles, then the Boston Red Sox, and finally the New York Yankees (who won seven pennants and four World Championships from 1920 to 1933, when he was on the team), and hit 714 official home runs.

And thanks to the efforts of the batboy, Maurice Fleishman, a historic marker was erected by the state at the site in Fayetteville where the Babe hit that first home run.

N★C Strange . . . but true

When Playing Baseball Cost Dearly

A young man who played in the minor leagues during the early years of professional baseball in the Tarheel State became famous—despite being a mediocre player, to say the least. As first baseman and pitcher, he won only nine games and lost ten, and his batting average was .253. Originally from Pennsylvania, this player of Native American heritage joined the team in Rocky Mount in 1909 to play in the Eastern Carolina Association.

Several years later, in 1912, Jim Thorpe went on to win two gold medals in the decathlon and pentathlon in the Olympics in Stockholm, Sweden. His not-so-successful attempt to play professional baseball, however, would cost him dearly. Officials heard of his having played in the minor leagues, and in 1913 took back the two Olympic gold medals Thorpe had won, because Olympic athletes were required to be amateurs.

Thorpe later played halfback for the New York Giants, and was declared America's Greatest Football Player of the Half Century in 1950. Members of the press named him Outstanding Athlete of the Twentieth Century.

The Olympic medals were returned to Thorpe's family in 1982, long after his death in 1953.

Family NASCAR Dynasties

The racing world seems to attract competitors who make their profession a family tradition, such as the Petty and Earnhardt families.

The Petty family is full of NASCAR professional racers. Patriarch Lee Petty, from Randolph County, won fifty-four NASCAR Grand Nationals and the title of NASCAR Grand National Driving Champion three times. His son, Richard, and grandson, Kyle, also are racers, as was Kyle's son, Adam Petty.

Lee Petty passed away April 5, 2000, at age eighty-six. On May 12, 2000, tragedy again struck the Pettys when nineteen-year-old great-grandson Adam died in a practice run.

A Kannapolis native, Dale Earnhardt learned the thrill of racing from his father Ralph, who amassed 350 victories in his own twenty-three-year racing career. Making his own debut at Charlotte Motor Speedway in 1975, Dale was named Rookie of the Year for his stellar performances on the track. In his second year of racing he won his first Winston Cup Series—and this was the first of seven such victories.

He was called "the Intimidator" for his fearless and aggressive racing style, and continued to win victories and gain fame during his career. He died on the racetrack in an accident during the last lap of the Daytona 500 on February 18, 2001. Ironically, the race was won by his teammate Michael Waltrip, with his son Dale Earnhardt Jr. coming in second. Dale Earnhardt Jr. continues to race, and his racing team is based near Mooresville.

Did You Know? For those who can't get enough of NASCAR and all things related, two museums in North Carolina are dedicated to the world of auto racing: the North Carolina Racing Hall of Fame in Mooresville and the Richard Petty Museum in Level Cross.

The Richard Petty Museum in Level Cross has a remarkable collection of NASCAR treasures. (COURTESY N.C. DIVISION OF TOURISM, FILM, AND SPORTS DEVELOPMENT)

N★C **Strange . . . but true**

This Young Fan Is Really a Kid!

NASCAR fans have been making a pilgrimage to the town of Interlachen, Florida, to see a young kid born in March 2002. This "kid" is really just that—a goat. What makes this fawn-colored Nubian kid such a curiosity is that she was born with a very distinctive number 3 on her side.

"An image of a ghost is on her other side," says owner Jerry Pierson, a farmer and huge NASCAR fan. "When she was born, we thought immediately of Dale Earnhardt and named the goat Lil' Dale." Since her birth, the quiet life of the Pierson family has been all but that, with the media spreading the word of the four-legged Earnhardt fan. "She was even given a spread in a recent issue of *Sports Illustrated*," Pierson says.

Dale Earnhardt fans flock to Interlachen, Florida, to marvel at Lil' Dale, the goat born with the number 3 on her side. (COURTESY JERRY PIERSON)

He's About a Lot More Than "Air"

You probably know that Michael Jordan had a brilliant career with the Chicago Bulls and was named NBA Most Valuable Player of the Year five times. You may be familiar with his Nike commercials or his restaurants, such as Michael Jordan's 23 in Chapel Hill, featuring his retired number. You may know that he returned to play with the Washington Wizards and that he's a cigar aficionado. But Jordan is about more than business, competition, and basketball—he's got the heart of a philanthropist, which all started with his father and that father's love.

James R. Jordan was a family man. He often said that his family was his life, and showed this with the way he lived, caring for and spending time with his children, Deloris, Larry, Michael, and Roslyn, in Wilmington. A sign of greatness is in how those who have achieved success give back, and Michael Jordan has given back in several ways. In October 1996, after his father's death, Michael, his siblings, and his mother had a ribbon-cutting ceremony for the Jordan Institute for Families, part of the School of Social Work at the University of North Carolina in Chapel Hill. Michael Jordan's $1 million gift supplied seed money to support the work of the institute.

Jordan said at the dedication ceremonies that he felt "very blessed . . . to have had a family structure" that nurtured him and his siblings, and he added that many youngsters today lacked that home nurturing.

Michael Jordan's efforts have had a ripple effect: In November 1996 Jordan's teammates opened the James R. Jordan Boys and Girls Club and Family Life Center in Chicago to serve the children of the West Side community. The programs and services offered include education, employment skills training, a community health center, and more. And since Jordan started playing with the Wizards, he has pledged half of his earnings to the victims of the September 11, 2001 terrorist attacks on the United States.

Michael Jordan continues to be a role model to generations of children and adults because of the love he knew when he was brought up in North Carolina.

Not Tall Enough? Try This!

When Michael Jordan was a very young boy, he was dwarfed by some of the other players on the court. Discouraged, he asked his mother what he could do to make himself taller. She suggested two things: prayer and a dash of salt in his sneakers, to be done nightly. Who's to say it didn't work?

Guess Who? This young man from Hertford made his major league baseball debut in 1965, pitched five victorious World Series games with the Oakland Athletics and New York Yankees, won the 1974 American League Cy Young Award for the best pitcher of the year, and was inducted into the Baseball Hall of Fame.

Who was this athlete? Jim "Catfish" Hunter.

N★C SPORTS TRIVIA I

Q. Where was North Carolina's first jockey club?

A. Wilmington.

Q. What county is famous for its equestrian events, such as the Tryon Riding and Hunt Club Blockhouse Steeplechase (which has been occurring for nearly sixty years)?

A. Polk County.

Q. What Wilmington native won the 1976 Olympic gold medal in boxing and five world boxing titles, won twenty-five of thirty-six matches by knockouts, and was inducted into the International Boxing Hall of Fame in 1997?

A. Sugar Ray Leonard.

Q. What North Carolina museum exhibits hundreds of hand-carved decoy ducks?

A. The Core Sound Waterfowl Museum, on Harker's Island.

Q. What two teams played the first "scientific" game of football (according to intercollegiate rules) in North Carolina in 1888?

A. University of North Carolina played Trinity College (now Duke University) at the State Fairgrounds in Raleigh. Trinity won, 16-0.

Q. In what year was the first-ever intercollegiate football game between black colleges?

A. 1892, with Salisbury's Livingstone College hosting Biddle Institute (now Johnson C. Smith Institute). Livingstone won, 4-0.

Q. When was the first intercollegiate basketball game in the Tarheel State?

A. February 6, 1906, between Wake Forest and Guilford. Guilford won, 26-19.

Q. What University of North Carolina coach developed a football team that became known as the "Team of a Million Backs"?

A. Chuck Collins, coach from 1926 to 1933.

Q. What collegiate football team gave the University of North Carolina its only defeat in 1935, preventing it from reaching the Rose Bowl?

A. Duke University. The two teams have one of the fiercest rivalries in the South.

Q. *What player in the Negro Leagues was from Rocky Mount and nicknamed "the black Lou Gehrig"?*

A. *Walter (Buck) Leonard, who played with the Baltimore Stars, the Brooklyn Royal Giants, and the Homestead (Pennsylvania) Grays, and was inducted into the National Baseball Hall of Fame in 1972.*

Guess Who? This golfer with personality-plus was a student at Wake Forest University and won the first Atlantic Coast Conference tournament in 1954. Now he designs golf courses—and still plays, not so much for the money or the fame, but for his fans.

Who is this charismatic Tarheel golf champ? Arnold Palmer.

Challenging Color Codes and Exceeding the Odds

Today, thanks to African American golfers who in the 1950s challenged the PGA's rule prohibiting them from competing in the "Game of Kings," no one can be proclaimed ineligible because of race. One of the early golfers who fought against racial discrimination on the links and off was golfing great Charlie Sifford.

Sifford was a Charlotte native who fell in love with the game the moment he saw his first course. He became a caddy and learned the game from the greens up. Although he wanted to compete with players on equal turf, doing so was not easy.

He and his friends were barred from playing at country clubs, which didn't allow nonwhites. Caddies were allowed to play one day a week, however, and the young Charlie jumped at every such opportunity. Also, after hours he and his friends would sneak back onto the links, hitting balls until they were run off by the golf pros or security. That helped Charlie learn to play fast—although he never got to pay much attention to his putting, a part of the game he knew was his weakness. Putting takes time and concentration, and playing under such circumstances wouldn't allow for either.

In the late 1940s, three African American golfers (Ted Rhodes, Bill Spiller, and Madison Gunter) brought suit against the PGA for barring nonwhites from PGA competition. The PGA responded by dropping the nonwhite rule—but declared the tournaments invitation-only, effectively barring African Americans.

Sifford endured countless humiliations while he was trying to play the game he loved. In the early days, he wasn't allowed to dine in the country club restaurants and took more meals than he cared to in the locker room. Sometimes he wasn't allowed to use any of the facilities where he competed—including the locker rooms and the restrooms. He didn't let any of this stop him.

In August 1955 he and fellow golfer Ted Rhodes played the Canadian Open, which had no race barrier. Sifford played well enough to feel more confident about becoming a professional golfer. The next year, he signed up to play the Rhode Island Open, and won his first "white" tournament. It wasn't PGA, but it was a foot in the door. Now Sifford was determined to enter and win a sure-enough PGA tournament. First he had to become a member.

Sifford went through legal channels to force the PGA to change its membership rules, which as recently as 1961 only allowed whites. The rule was removed in 1962, but holding a member's card still wouldn't get him through the country club gates. Sifford decided to go through the back door by competing in open tournaments (ones that were open to all, regardless of membership or rank).

In 1961, Sifford signed on to play as the first African American golfer in the PGA Greater Greensboro Open. This was during the time of lunch-counter sit-ins and the beginning of the civil rights movement, and Charlie Sifford was right in the middle of it. The night before he was to play for the first time on a PGA course, he got a phone call. It was a death threat, with racial slurs thrown in.

On the greens that day, he was hounded by hecklers. Sifford kept his cool and concentrated on the game. He finished, amazingly enough, at 72, only one over par—but realized he would be the one to open the door to other black golfers, and the difficulties he would face would mean sacrificing his full potential as a golfer. That first year as a PGA rookie, he wrote in his autobiography, was one unlike that of any other rookie. He went on to win the Hartford Open in 1967, becoming the first African American to win in PGA competition.

As he wrote in his memoirs, all he wanted to do was play. Thanks to Charlie Sifford, today's golf greats don't have to break down racial barriers and the competition is wide open in the "Game of Kings."

Did You Know? The Ferrell brothers from Greensboro are among some of the best-known baseball greats. George had a brilliant career in the minors, catcher Rick played in nearly two thousand games in eighteen years, and pitcher Wes had a record of 193-128 with a no-hitter in 1931. Rick Ferrell was inducted into the National Baseball Hall of Fame in Cooperstown, New York, in 1984.

The Queen of NC State Basketball

Born in Gibsonville, Kay Yow was one of four athletic children. She and her sisters, Debbie and Susan, all played basketball in high school (and all wore the Number 14 jersey, which has since been retired), and her brother, Ronnie, played football. Yow was dismayed, however, to find little opportunity to play basketball in college. Very few colleges offered varsity women's sports, let alone athletic scholarships. Yow satisfied her athletic streak and natural ability by playing softball.

Yow majored in English, then earned a master's degree in physical education and landed a job teaching English at Allen Jay High School in High Point. In 1964 a position opened for the girl's basketball team coach and Yow jumped at the opportunity. She realized she could combine her teaching talents with her athletic ability, and coached the team to four straight league championships, the highest honor available to a girl's basketball team in North Carolina in the 1960s.

From there, she coached at her alma mater, Gibsonville, then took a coaching job at Elon College, where from 1971 to 1975 she had a 57-19 record and led her teams to two state championships. In 1975 she became head coach of the women's basketball team at North Carolina State University. She has been leading the "Wolfpack Women" ever since.

Yow has inspired her players to excellence, both on and off court. Her team won the silver medal in the 1981 World University Games. In 1986 her teams took gold medals in the World Championships and the Goodwill Games. In 1988 her team won the gold medal in the Olympic Games—probably especially satisfying for Yow as women's basketball wasn't even an Olympic sport until 1976.

Some of her achievements have included breaking the five hundred–win mark in 1996 and being named the Women's Basketball Coach of the Year by *College Sports News* when she directed the Wolfpack Women to the Final Four in 1998. She received the President and Mrs. George Bush Community Impact Award, and in 2000 was inducted into the Women's Basketball Hall of Fame in Knoxville, Tennessee.

Coach Kay Yow led the "Wolfpack Women" to victory and helped make women's basketball the high-profile sport it is today.
(COURTESY N.C. STATE UNIVERSITY)

Today, Kay Yow is one of the most admired and respected coaches in international and collegiate basketball. Perhaps she didn't realize that when she left the English classroom to coach, she would help make women's basketball a high-profile sport.

Guess Who? This Wilmington native was a strong-armed quarterback with North Carolina State, where he was recognized twice as an All-American. He played for the Rams for eleven seasons, was named NFL's MVP in 1969, and played five seasons for the Philadelphia Eagles. Now he's a radio and TV personality, and has appeared in several movies. Who is this man? Roman Gabriel.

Sir Archie and the Culture of Horse Racing

In 1805 in Virginia, a foal destined for fame was born. His parents were of English racing stock, and his mother had won the English Derby in 1780. Eventually named Sir Archie, the horse went through several owners and eventually arrived on Marmaduke Johnson's plantation in Warren County, North Carolina, where he trained for the 1808 Virginia season. In that season, he beat all other competition on hooves.

His final race of the season was at the Scotland Neck racetrack in Halifax County, and because Sir Archie was racing an unbeaten horse named Blank, no one thought Sir Archie could win. When Sir Archie won, the race became the most famous in North Carolina. Sir Archie, of course, became famous as well.

When Sir Archie had beaten all the competition and no takers answered to a challenge, Johnson sold him. After several different owners, Sir Archie finally came to spend the rest of his life at William Amis's plantation, Mowfield, in Northhampton County. Here, from 1816 to 1831, Sir Archie may have spent his happiest days. During these years he was a stud horse, and with his racing and genetic history he was quite popular with the owners of mares.

So popular was he that during those years, Sir Archie sired more than four hundred sons and daughters, earning the name Foundation Sire of the American Thoroughbred. Sir Archie's progeny carried on his racing ability to such an extent that by 1827, Northern racing clubs began to exclude the "Roanoke Racers" from their events.

For Some "Reel" Adventures

North Carolina has some of the best fishing to be had, both on the coast and along its forty thousand-odd miles of rivers and streams. You can try to beat these freshwater records:

★ **Bodie bass:** 17 pounds, 7 ounces, Lake Chatuge, 1996

★ **Smallmouth buffalo:** 88 pounds, Lake Wylie, 1993

★ **Blue catfish:** 80 pounds, Cape Fear River, 1999

★ **Brown trout:** 24 pounds, 10 ounces, Nantahala River, 1998

Those who love fishing ocean waters could try for the World All-Tackle Records (a world record regardless of what type of tackle used). Those include

★ **Bluefish:** 31 pounds, 12 ounces, Cape Hatteras, 1972

★ **Red drum:** 94 pounds, 2 ounces, Hatteras Island, 1984

★ **Spanish mackerel:** 13 pounds, Ocracoke Inlet, 1987

So whether you fish with a fly rod, casting rod, or deep-sea rig, try your luck. Just wear your lucky fishing hat!

N★C Strange . . . but true

National Baseball Hall of Famer Enos "Country" Slaughter, a native of Roxboro, became a noted outfielder in the 1940s and 1950s. He had a lifetime batting average of .300 and an especially strong throwing arm. Slaughter gave credit for his prowess in throwing to a boyhood hobby unrelated to baseball. When he was a young boy, he hunted rabbits—by throwing rocks at them!

N★C SPORTS TRIVIA II

Q. Who was the first football All-American in North Carolina?

A. Fred Crawford, who played at Duke and was All-American in 1933.

Q. What Duke University football coach turned the Blue Devils into a winning machine and produced the team of 1938 known as the Iron Duke?

A. Wallace Wade, head football coach at Duke from 1931 to 1941.

Q. What football great played at Duke University during the mid-1930s, played both pro baseball and pro football between 1937 and 1946, and was named the NFL's Most Valuable Player in 1940?

A. Clarence (Ace) Parker, who was enshrined in the Pro Football Hall of Fame in 1972.

Q. Who are the only two siblings to be awarded the Cy Young Award?

A. Jim and Gaylord Perry, Williamston natives.

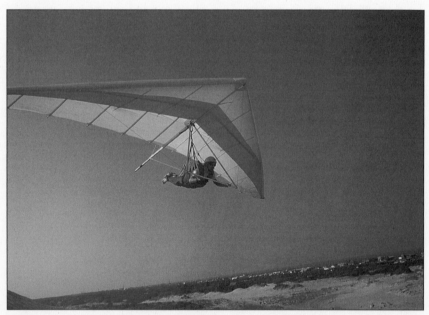

Q. *Where is the annual three-day Hang Gliding Spectacular held?*

A. *Jockey's Ridge in Nag's Head, the tallest sand dune in the United States (more than one hundred feet).*

(COURTESY N.C. DIVISION OF TOURISM, FILM, AND SPORTS DEVELOPMENT)

Q. Who finished second in the Heisman Trophy voting in 1948 and 1949 and has been called the most well-known football player in North Carolina history? (Hint: he played for Coach Carl Snavely at the University of North Carolina in Chapel Hill.)

A. All-American Charlie (Choo-Choo) Justice.

Q. What is nicknamed the "Mecca of Motor Sports"?

A. Lowe's Motor Speedway, near Charlotte.

Q. What town won the 1940 Little World Series, a game sponsored by the American Legion and played by Little League ballplayers?

A. Albemarle, who defeated San Diego, 9-8.

Q. What National Basketball Hall of Famer from Cleveland County, who played for North Carolina State and the Denver Nuggets, is called "the Michael Jordan of the 1970s"?

A. David Thompson.

Q. What North Carolinian invented hang gliding?

A. Francis Rogallo, who lives near Jockey's Ridge.

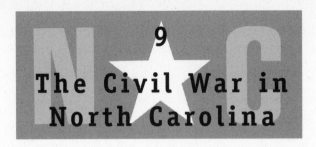

9
The Civil War in North Carolina

The Tarheels: First, Farthest, and Last

A Civil War saying popular in North Carolina was "First at Bethel, farthest at Gettysburg, and last at Appomattox." Here's why.

The first Confederate soldier to die in a Civil War battle was a North Carolinian. Henry L. Wyatt of the First North Carolina died on June 10, 1861, in the Battle of Big Bethel, an early Confederate victory. Wyatt's commanding officer, Colonel John B. Magruder, called him "a brave soldier and devoted patriot," and Wyatt was buried in Richmond and his tombstone inscribed "First at Bethel." There's a statue of Wyatt on the Capitol grounds in Raleigh.

"Farthest at Gettysburg" was added to the saying when the Twenty-sixth North Carolina, under

Henry L. Wyatt's death at the Battle of Big Bethel was the first Confederate loss of the Civil War. (COURTESY N.C. DEPT. OF CULTURAL RESOURCES)

Colonel Zebulon Vance, suffered the most Confederate casualties at that battle.

"Last at Appomattox" became part of the credo when the brigade of North Carolinians under General William Ruffin Cox and the Army of Northern Virginia fired the last shots of the war in the vicinity of the Appomattox Courthouse on April 9, 1865, the day General Robert E. Lee surrendered.

N★C Strange . . . but true

The Spy and the Missing Gold

Rose O'Neal Greenhow was a Wilmington native and from all accounts, beautiful. She was also a spy for the Confederacy. After writing a book about her covert experiences, she was returning from England in 1864 aboard the *Condor* with $2,000 in gold. The gold was from the sales of her book, and she planned to donate it to the Confederate cause.

The ship approached New Inlet to try to anchor and wait out a storm, but was met by a Union ship, the USS *Niphon*. The *Niphon* gave chase and the *Condor* ran aground.

Rose had already spent time in a Northern prison for being a spy, and she was not about to be captured and imprisoned again. Rose cast off in a small dinghy, gold and all. No sooner was she in the turbulent waters than the boat capsized. Rose drowned and her body washed up later on the shores of Fort Fisher. She was draped for burial in a Confederate flag and laid out in Wilmington. Rose was buried with full military honors in Oakdale Cemetery, where you can see her tombstone.

A mystery persists about the gold. Some say that the gold was sewn into the seams of her dress or around her neck, and caused her to drown. Others say Rose's gold lies at the bottom of the Atlantic near New Inlet, and that the spirit of the ill-fated spy continues to haunt the area, looking for her missing treasure.

New Bern, Cover-Girl City of the War

Just after the Battle of New Bern on March 14, 1862, Federal troops occupied the city until the end of the war. That might have seemed to be a terrible fate for the loyal Confederate citizens of New Bern, but it ultimately saved their town from torching and pillaging. Because it was occupied so early in the conflict, New Bern was spared from destruction. It was so untouched by war's devastation that it was the most photographed Southern city during the war—and remains a picture-perfect town.

The Civil War Meets Modern Archaeology

As soon as North Carolina seceded from the Union, Tarheels realized that they needed to protect the coast, and set to work constructing forts along the banks. On Beacon Island, soldiers and volunteers constructed a fort in May 1861 from barrels of sand and many layers of sod. Dubbed Fort Ocracoke, it was armed with two cannons called Columbiads, four eight-inch shell guns, and fourteen smooth-bore cannons. It was also shored up

An artist depicted Fort Ocracoke after it was partially destroyed by Confederate forces in August 1861. (COURTESY OCRACOKE PRESERVATION SOCIETY)

with ballast stones as a breakwater to prevent the tides from washing it out. Fort Ocracoke was planned to be a coastal bastion of the Confederacy, but history would have it otherwise.

In August 1861 Union armies assaulted and took over nearby Fort Hatteras and Fort Clark. Realizing the inevitable fate of their own fort, the Confederates manning Fort Ocracoke set fire to her gun platforms, then fled in a gunboat. Union soldiers vandalized and burned what was left of the earthen fort. Time did the rest, and early in the twentieth century, the remains of Fort Ocracoke and Beacon Island itself were submerged under the waters of Ocracoke Inlet.

In 1998, 137 years later, charter boat captain Donald Austin spotted what he thought was a shipwreck in the inlet, and tipped off divers working for Surface Interval Diving. This Beaufort-based nonprofit marine archaeo-logical company was searching for the pirate Blackbeard's sunken ship, and thought Austin might have spotted the famed *Queen Anne's Revenge*.

What they found were the remains of Fort Ocracoke. Ballast stones, pieces of pottery, and other debris were tested and determined to be Civil War artifacts from the doomed earthen fortress.

In April 2000 the marine archaeologists who discovered the remains held a ceremony to commemorate the history behind the fort and to honor the soldiers who had served from Ocracoke and Portsmouth Islands. Today you can see the artifacts on display in a museum operated by the Ocracoke Preservation Society. Offshore, captains conducting small private boat tours point out the historic submerged site to their passengers.

Did You Know? General William T. Sherman and his ravenous troops left behind one chicken after besieging Raleigh in 1865— and you can still see it today! It's a brass chicken, atop the weather vane on the roof of Christ Episcopal Church, downtown.

Cherokee in the Civil War

Thomas's Legion was a Civil War regiment credited with firing the last shots of the Civil War in North Carolina. The legion was raised by William Holland Thomas, who lived among the Cherokee in the mountains of North Carolina. When the enforced march now known as the Trail of Tears was imminent, Thomas persuaded President Andrew Jackson to allow some of the tribe to stay in the mountains. As Thomas was an attorney and state senator, his request carried weight.

When the Civil War broke out, Thomas recruited his tribal friends to join him. At the beginning, "Thomas's Legion" consisted of about 130 Cherokee soldiers, but this number quickly grew to include more Cherokee and also their white mountaineer neighbors.

Varying historical accounts claim that Thomas's Legion scalped some of its opponents. Whether these tales were true or not, Thomas's Legion's reputation for ferocity spread like wildfire, and the group retains the distinction of being one of the Confederacy's most distinguished fighting units.

Because it was composed mostly of Cherokee, Thomas's Legion is now honored in the Museum of the Cherokee Indian in Cherokee.

Thomas's Legion of Cherokee Indian Confederate Veterans pose for a photograph at a post-war reunion. (COURTESY N.C. DEPT. OF CULTURAL RESOURCES)

"Waterloo Teeth" and Civil War Dentistry

Before the advent of today's dentures, teeth were more often pulled than saved, and many different types of materials were used to make dentures. Bone, ivory, and wood were carved to make rudimentary replacements.

Sometimes, too, human teeth were used. Called Waterloo Teeth because they were often gathered from dead soldiers as they lay on the battlefield, the Civil War resulted in the manufacture of many "real" dentures. During the war, entire barrelsful of teeth were taken from dead soldiers and shipped to England.

Did You Know? The flag of the Confederacy was designed by Orren R. Smith of Franklin.

The Brief Reign of the Smithville Home Guard

Like many towns during the Civil War, Smithville saw a need for a Home Guard. Home Guards were created to protect the town's inhabitants and their possessions while so many of the able-bodied men were off fighting.

In late May 1861, the concerned residents met at the courthouse and voted to create a Home Guard composed of all those men who were not able to go to war. A Smithville citizen named John Bell was appointed captain, although a historian later said Bell must have been too "good natured and not likely to enforce any military discipline whatsoever."

When the newly elected Captain Bell suggested that the Guard meet the next morning for its first drill, some of the elderly "guardsmen" proposed that they bring stools so when they got tired, they could sit and rest. Following this suggestion, perhaps in an effort to prove who was in charge, Bell ordered the Guard to attention and had them march around town. But as each guardsman passed near his residence, he disappeared.

As the ranks were so alarmingly diminished, Bell did the only thing he probably could do, given the circumstances and his own personality. He made a motion to dissolve the Home Guard, which was unanimously carried—by all who were left to hear the motion, anyway.

This may well be the shortest-lived Home Guard unit in the entire Civil War.

The CSS *Neuse*

This ironclad vessel was the hope of the Confederacy, one of twenty-two such vessels commissioned by the navy. Flat-bottomed, measuring 158 feet long and 34 feet wide, CSS *Neuse* resembled a barge more than a warship. Her mission was to recapture Union-held New Bern, and help the Confederacy stem the tide of war. But the *Neuse* was destined never to see action south of Kinston, where she was constructed. First she was beset by construction delays; then low tides and insufficient ground support prevented her from seeing much combat to the south.

Her fatal blow was in March 1865, when Union soldiers took over Kinston. As Confederate soldiers were obliged to do when the enemy was

The hull of the CSS Neuse, *one of only three Confederate ironclads to be recovered and displayed, can be seen in Kinston.* (COURTESY CSS *NEUSE* STATE HISTORIC SITE)

threatening to take over one of their own vessels, the sailors of the *Neuse* set her afire. The *Neuse* sank in the Neuse River, and there she lay until raised in 1964. The hull was transported to what is now the CSS *Neuse* State Historic Site in Kinston, where you can see her today.

The *Neuse* is one of only three Confederate ironclads ever recovered and displayed. At the historic site are the remains of the hull and other artifacts that relate to this tragic era in America's past.

The Tragic Story of the Harper House

The Battle of Bentonville in the final year of the Civil War was a long and bloody one, and the climax of the Carolinas Campaign. What happened to the people who lived near these battlegrounds, however, is not often considered.

John and Amy Harper lived with their six children in a two-story home near the site. Once the battle commenced, their home was turned from a peaceful haven into a makeshift field hospital. The house was filled with the screams and moans of wounded and dying soldiers. One historian estimated that five hundred soldiers were brought in during a twenty-four-hour period. One officer, Lieutenant Colonel William Douglas Hamilton of the Ninth Ohio Cavalry, said the hospital "resembled a slaughterhouse. A dozen surgeons and their attendants in their shirtsleeves stood at rude benches cutting off arms and legs and throwing them out of the windows, where they lay scattered on the grass."

Today, you can visit and tour the Bentonville Battleground State Historic Site and the Harper House, on the grounds of the site of the last full-scale Confederate offensive.

School's Not So Tough After All!

The first students to go into battle during the Civil War were teenage cadets in a military school. Fifteen such cadets, enrolled in the North Carolina Military Academy in Charlotte, took part in the battle of Big Bethel, Virginia, on June 10, 1861. This was also the first significant military clash of the war, and was a Confederate victory.

N★C Stran©e . . . but true

Way Before Bonnie and Clyde

Sam and Keith Blalock, hailing from the Grandfather Mountain area, enlisted with the Confederate Army's Twenty-sixth North Carolina Regiment early in the war. Other soldiers noted that the brothers were close and the slighter brother avoided skinny-dipping.

Now history knows that Keith's brother Sam was not really his brother, and not really "Sam," either. This person was in fact Keith's wife, Malinda.

Although history has noted women who served the war effort as nurses, many people don't realize that women—perhaps hundreds on both sides—took part in the Civil War as soldiers. They cut their hair, bound their curves, and spoke as deeply as possible. Some did it to be near a sweetheart or avenge the death of a loved one. Others did it for adventure.

Sam Blalock, however, was wounded in battle, which led to the discovery that "Sam" was actually Malinda. Upon her immediate release from the Confederate Army, Keith came down with severe poison sumac and was released (some say he did this on purpose). Keith, in fact, had originally enlisted with the Confederates to be near Malinda and protect her, although both sympathized with the Union. Historians speculate that they joined the Twenty-sixth North Carolina Regiment so that they could get near enough to Union forces to desert the Confederate Army.

Following their exit from the Confederate military, Malinda and Keith joined Union forces as scouts and raiders. They also became something of a Bonnie-and-Clyde team, happily bushwhacking civilians, soldiers, and even their neighbors for several years in the hollows and trails around Grandfather Mountain. Malinda died in her sleep in 1903 and Keith in a handcar accident in 1913, in Hickory. They are buried in Avery County in the Montezuma Community Cemetery.

The Blalocks have ensured their place in history because they are the only husband and wife to have fought side by side—and on *both* sides of the Civil War!

Lion-hearted Flusser

Southern-born Charles Williamson Flusser was handsome, with dark hair and steely eyes. He was also unmoving in his convictions, and when the Civil War broke out, his loyalties remained with the Union, although his family sympathized with the South. Despite family friction because of his Union steadfastness, the 1853 Annapolis graduate had a single burning goal during the war: to captain a steam-powered warship.

His ambitions were soon realized. When Virginia seceded from the Union in 1861, after some "persuasion" from the Confederate military, the commander of the Navy Yard in Norfolk relinquished his control of the shipbuilding facility to the Confederates. This was important for the Confederate Army, which needed a shipbuilding facility.

The Union Army knew that by claiming the Norfolk shipyard, the Confederate Army would soon take the battle to the sea and into waterways, especially around and into North Carolina. North Carolina's Roanoke Island was considered to be of strategic importance; by seizing it, the Union Army could take control of the railroad connection between the North and the South. A plan unfolded to seize the island, take control of nearby New Bern, and either take or destroy the Wilmington and Weldon railways.

The stage was set for naval conflict, and in 1862 Flusser was given command of his own Union gunboat. He gained admiration from even seasoned naval officers for his handling of the USS *Commodore Perry* in the battles of Roanoke Island and Elizabeth City. Flusser was said to be so talented and crafty a seaman that he could float his seven-hundred-ton gunboat on either a "wet sponge or a heavy dew," traversing the most shallow waterways into North Carolina and routing out the enemy. He became known as Lion-hearted Flusser.

What makes this story remarkable is the craft Flusser used to wage his watery North Carolina campaign—a former Staten Island ferryboat. After testing its seaworthiness, Flusser regarded it with no small degree of disgust. "This steamer though a very good one for river and sound work, has proved utterly unfit for service at sea," Flusser wrote to his mother. "I turned back yesterday . . . from a sea in which I should have felt perfectly secure in an ordinary ship boat or small row boat."

With Flusser at the helm of the most unlikely warship and former ferry boat *Commodore Perry*, he proved himself beyond all doubt a capable naval officer. Later in the war he was put in charge of real gunboats, and helped the Union Army make a successful invasion and conquest of coastal North Carolina. He died in the Battle of Plymouth, on April 19, 1864.

The Gibraltar of the South

Known during the Civil War as "the Gibraltar of the South" because it was deemed unassailable, Fort Fisher was the largest earthwork fortification in the South and in a perfect spot to protect Confederate interests. Fort Fisher was built overlooking the Cape Fear River on one side and the Atlantic Ocean on the other, and it protected blockade runners who used the port of Wilmington. When all other ports were effectively cut off from the Confederacy, the last surviving port of Wilmington and its protector, Fort Fisher, became crucial. Union forces attacked Fort Fisher not once but twice, in late 1864 and early 1865, making the fort the target of the most extensive naval bombardment of the Civil War.

Six weeks after the fall of Fort Fisher and the subsequent surrender of Wilmington, General Robert E. Lee surrendered at the Appomattox Courthouse. The Gibraltar of the South had become another statistic of the Civil War.

After the Civil War, Fort Fisher was allowed to fall into

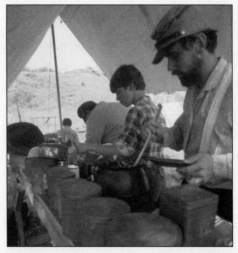

Civil War reenactors line up for a meal at Fort Fisher State Historic Site. (COURTESY N.C. DIVISION OF TRAVEL AND TOURISM)

disrepair and was left to the ravages of the sea. Several attempts were made to save it, as the beach continued to encroach and nature and time began to reclaim the area.

Finally, in 1958, what remained of Fort Fisher became a state historic site. A visitors' center there contains interpretive exhibits and artifacts from sunken blockade runners in the area.

Just Can't Keep a Confederate Soldier Down

Captain Richard Keough was of Company H, Sixty-eighth Regiment, North Carolina Troops, which in April 1863 was holed up at "the Widow Gascon's house" at Poll's Fishery near the mouth of the Chowan River. Since March 1863, Keough had been wanted for the Edenton ambush of a member of the First Regiment of New York Mounted Rifles. Lieutenant Charles Flusser and his men captured Keough and other Confederate soldiers and took them to Plymouth to the Provost Marshal.

Amazingly, Keough was released after taking the Oath of Allegiance to the United States—then promptly found his way back to his own company, to fight again!

Fighting in the Buff

On more than one occasion, soldiers on both sides were obliged to go *au naturel*, such as when fording a deep creek. They'd roll their clothing around their guns and carry them over their heads when crossing rivers. Other times they'd be without clothes when bathing in the rivers or trying to wash lice off their bodies. Sometimes they would use nudity as an unusual tactical element to surprise the enemy. Fighting unclad soldiers could be discombobulating enough to gain victory.

One such instance was on July 26, 1863, when Confederate General Matt W. Ransom gave the soldiers of the Twenty-fourth North Carolina permission to clean up in a millpond. Suddenly, several hundred soldiers in blue descended upon them, and Ransom's men were obliged to fend off their attackers despite being nude. The Union soldiers tried to rout the

Confederates at Boone's Mill, but after a five-hour battle, gave up. E. M. McCook, a Union general, wrote in his journal about such battles "in the buff" as "certainly one of the funniest sights of the war."

N★C Strange . . . but true

The Tale of an Officer and a Gentleman

During the surrender to Union forces, Confederate Major James Reilly, the last commander of Fort Fisher, handed over his saber to Captain E. Lewis Moore from Massachusetts.

After the loss of Fort Fisher, Reilly was a prisoner of war for four months in Fort Delaware. Upon taking the Oath of Allegiance to the federal government, Reilly returned to the Wilmington area and spent his remaining years farming and enjoying a celebrity status for his courage during the fight over the fort.

In 1893 he unexpectedly received a special gift from the captain to whom he had surrendered thirty years before. Lewis had located Reilly through newspaper inquiries, and returned what Reilly had given him as he stood at Battery Buchanan and surrendered Fort Fisher.

Reilly died peacefully the year after receiving the saber he had relinquished to Lewis at the end of the battle of Fort Fisher. The saber, on loan from Reilly's descendants, is on exhibit at the Fort Fisher State Historic Site.

Hard Times in the Carolinas

During the Civil War, civilians as well as soldiers had to make do with what was on hand, or create substitutions. What's amazing is that some of these remedies and recipes are still in use today.

Women made apple pie without apples by mixing any kind of sweetener, butter, and nutmeg with a bowl of moistened crackers (*that's* where that recipe came from!). Coffee substitute was made from roasted acorns and a small amount of bacon fat or lard, or dried sassafras leaves and ground okra seeds. Coffee drinkers in the Confederate states stretched that bean by adding wild chicory—and you can still find some brands of coffee-chicory blends on grocery shelves today.

Dysentery could be cured with salt and vinegar, boiled together. One grandmother remembers that old folks in her family used charcoal cooled from the fire, then pounded and mixed with milk and turpentine to treat scarlet fever and diphtheria.

Did You Know? "Swoosh" or "sloosh" was an unusual campfire concoction made by Confederate soldiers: they ground corn with their rifle butts, mixed the corn with bacon drippings, molded it around their bayonets, and baked it in the campfire.

When Even the Bravest Man Wept

General Braxton Bragg assigned Confederate Major Pollock B. Lee the emotionally charged task of surrendering the city of Charlotte to Federal troops at the end of the war. Lee had always been a stalwart soldier, not given to emotional outbursts, but a comrade wrote of him that day, "It was the only time I ever saw him let fall a tear."

Sunken History

Of all the Civil War sites in the Tarheel State, perhaps the most historically valuable is under water—three hundred feet of water. On New Year's Eve 1862, the Union's first ironclad ship, USS *Monitor*, sank along with many of her crew off the coast of Cape Hatteras.

The *Monitor* had recently battled the Confederate ironclad the *Merrimack* (also known as the *Virginia*), off the coast of Hampton Roads, Virginia. The battle ended in a stalemate, and the *Monitor* set sail for Beaufort to help the Union blockade beat back the Confederate blockade runners.

The *Monitor* was not exactly a sleek, smoothly running vessel. She had been nicknamed "Cheesebox on a Raft" because of her poor maneuverability and how low and clumsily she rode in the water. She was being towed to Beaufort by the steamship *Rhode Island* when tragedy befell.

As can happen in the Outer Banks, stormy weather struck almost without warning. The unruly ocean took up where the *Merrimack* had left off. The *Monitor* began to take on water, foundering early in the evening. Around midnight, as the *Rhode Island* was attempting to rescue the *Monitor's* crew, she sank, taking sixteen men down with her.

No one knew the exact spot where the *Monitor* lay on the ocean floor, and for over one hundred years her whereabouts remained a mystery. Finally, in 1973, a Duke University research team discovered the vessel upside down, on the sandy bottom of the ocean floor, 240 feet below the surface and sixteen miles southeast of Cape Hatteras. Attempts to bring her up were unsuccessful, but in 1998 the U.S. Navy, the Mariners' Museum (based in Newport News, Virginia), and NOAA (National Oceanic and Atmospheric Administration) began a five-year-long recovery effort. Over four hundred artifacts (including the engine, the propeller, a 160-ton revolving gun turret, and two large Dahlgren cannons weighing 150 tons each) have been recovered and are now on display at the Mariners' Museum.

The U.S. government placed the sunken *Monitor* remains on the National Register of Historic Places two years after she was discovered. In 1975 NOAA designated the *Monitor's* resting place on the ocean floor a National Marine Sanctuary—the first place in the United States to be so designated.

Did You Know? In 1840 a young Army officer was assigned to inspect the bastion of Fort Macon, near Beaufort. The fort was destined to become the site of one of the quickest battles of the Civil War in North Carolina, which lasted only eleven hours. The young officer had a destiny of his own—to become one of the most famous figures in the Civil War. His name was Robert E. Lee. (Fort Macon survived the war and is now the dramatic centerpiece of one of the state's most visited state parks.)

The Near-Death Experience of Zebulon Vance

Asheville native Zebulon Vance was practicing law and serving as a congressman in Washington, D.C., when news arrived of the start of the Civil War. Vance had been a staunch Union supporter, but he was dismayed by Lincoln's call for volunteers after the firing on Fort Sumter, and realized his true loyalties lay with the Confederacy. Vance resigned his congressional seat, returned home to the mountains, and gathered his own set of volunteer soldiers, who became known as the Rough and Ready Guards. Later they became part of the Twenty-sixth North Carolina, and Vance became their colonel.

The Twenty-sixth North Carolina's "baptism by fire" was at the Battle of New Bern on March 14, 1862. Fighting against Burnside and his more than eleven thousand men, Vance's retreat to New Bern was cut off. The only avenue of escape was through Bryce's Creek.

It had rained heavily before the fighting, but Vance probably didn't take this into account, and still thought it was a wading creek. "Follow me, men!" he shouted to his frightened troops, as he and his steed plunged into the creek. But Vance didn't come up—weighed down with uniform, boots, ammunition, sword, and pistol, he sank like the proverbial stone. Some of his men saved him from drowning, and the soldiers crossed the creek in a boat, eighteen at a time.

Although Vance's Twenty-sixth North Carolina would go

Although Colonel Zebulon Vance became governor after the war, he never lived down the story of his near-death experience at the Battle of New Bern.
(COURTESY N.C. DEPT. OF CULTURAL RESOURCES)

into history as having the most Confederate casualties at Gettysburg, and Vance would become governor of North Carolina, the humorous story of Vance's near-death experience followed him throughout the rest of his political career.

The life and times of Zebulon Vance are commemorated at the home of his birth in Weaverville. The reconstructed 1830s-era Zebulon Vance Birthplace is open to the public.

The Economy and the Blockade Runners

As the Civil War continued much longer than either side had anticipated, Federal forces closed port after Southern port, and both civilian and soldiers alike felt the sting. The greatest impact was on the Confederate inflation rate: in May 1861 a one-dollar gold piece in Richmond was worth $1.10 in Confederate currency. By the end of the war, however, that same gold piece cost $60 in Confederate money.

As inflation rose, exacerbated by paper money with little gold to back it, so did the cost of precious goods. Rod Gragg wrote in *Planters, Pirates, and Patriots* (Nashville: Rutledge Hill Press, 1994) that basic commodities such as soap either disappeared or became prohibitively expensive. Even a sewing needle became a fiercely protected treasure.

Times were desperate, and to answer the need of the people for clothing, medicines, ammunition, and arms, a new breed of businessman arose: the blockade runner. The blockade runners and their ships largely saved the army of northern Virginia from starvation and kept the war going long after it was expected to end.

Their ships were built to run silently yet powerfully through Federal blockades as they headed toward commercial trade with foreign ports. They were two hundred feet long, weighing four hundred to eight hundred tons, with perhaps as many as three funnels. Their shallow draft (five to eleven feet) made them excellent at slipping in and out of the smaller inlets usually left unguarded by Federal gunboats. The vessels were fore-and-aft side wheelers (boats with four paddle wheels, two on each side, at opposite ends), which made them capable of sailing in a zigzag course to evade their enemy. Although blockade running was extremely hazardous, many adventuresome sailors tried it, and by late 1862 blockade running had been elevated in Confederate eyes to a fine art.

One such vessel, the *Fanny and Jenny,* was known as the Queen of the Blockade Runners. Like many others, however, the *Fanny and Jenny* met her fate at the hands of Federal blockaders. In February 1864, after returning with war contraband from Bermuda, she was in Wrightsville Beach, headed toward Wilmington, when not one but two blockaders discovered her. After the blockade-running captain refused to comply with a warning to "Heave to," the blockaders peppered the iron-hulled ship with cannon and gunfire. All surviving hands leaped to lifeboats while the Confederate vessel sank.

Shortly after the sinking of the *Fanny and Jenny,* the last Confederate port of Wilmington was effectively sealed off when Union soldiers took nearby Fort Fisher on January 15, 1865. This had been the last open port for blockade runners, and suddenly the Confederate Army, most notably in northern Virginia, faced critical shortages of food and ammunition. It was the beginning of the end for the Southern states.

The *Fanny and Jenny* is still under the waters of the Atlantic, and rumors of sunken treasure have drawn divers to her. At certain times and tides of the year, she can be seen from the beaches at Topsail Island.

The *Fanny and Jenny* carried one treasure to her watery grave: a gold sword, inscribed *To General Robert E. Lee, from his British Sympathisers,* that had been placed in care of the captain. Doug Medlin of Topsail Island, who runs a fishing and dive shop called East Coast Sports, hopes to find this and other treasures. "The *Fanny and Jenny* as well as many other blockade-running ships are right near shore," he says, "although some of them have migrated with the shifting of the sands, or because of storms." For years, Medlin has taken teams of divers to the sunken hulls of the blockade runners, including the *Fanny and Jenny.* "We salvaged some lead ingots off the ship, and I found an old padlock," he says, "but I never have found any of the gold said to be on board, or anything like a sword."

So that means there's treasure off the coast, just under the water, waiting to be discovered.

N★C Stran©e . . . but true

A Coincidence Saved a Spy from Hanging

In the early days of the Civil War, a sixteen-year-old from Raleigh named William Donald Carmichael served in the Confederate Army. He was with his unit in Virginia when he and a few other soldiers were sent on a reconnaissance mission to check the size and position of a nearby Yankee encampment.

When Union scouts discovered his unit, several Union soldiers were wounded or killed, and all the Confederate soldiers killed except young Carmichael. He was taken prisoner and tried as a spy, as he and his contingent had been well behind Union lines.

The young man was sentenced to be hanged the following Friday. The preceding Wednesday afternoon as he sat in his cell, a group of men walked down the corridor. One of them spoke to him, asking him why he was imprisoned and what his fate was to be. "They're going to hang me on Friday, Mr. President," young Carmichael replied, for the man was Abe Lincoln himself.

Saying that the boy was "too young to hang," Abraham Lincoln immediately wrote a pardon for him. Shortly after this the young soldier was released in a prison exchange.

When the war was over, Carmichael practiced law in Virginia and from there went to New York, where he presented the first Gilbert and Sullivan Opera performed in this country at the Casino Theatre.

His grandson, William Donald "Billy" Carmichael, was comptroller of the University of North Carolina during the 1940s. Billy Carmichael often wondered about what brought Lincoln down that particular prison corridor on that particular day, to save the man who would become his grandfather, from the hangman's noose.

North Carolina's Own Underground Railroad

Levi Coffin was born in New Garden. Quaker by birth and rearing, Coffin grew up to disdain slavery and all it entailed.

Coffin became an activist in helping runaway slaves to freedom. The New Garden area had a Quaker boarding school, and the woods behind the school are said to have harbored many runaway slaves. Eventually the woods became filled with hiding places such as dug-out pits covered with leaves and hollow logs large enough to hold a fleeing, frightened fugitive from slavery.

One night, a slave owner tracked a runaway to Coffin's door. Although Quakers are said to be teetotalers, Coffin plied the man with whiskey while the slave fled to another safe house. By the time the slave owner sobered up, he had forgotten why he had journeyed to New Garden—and the slave was on his way to freedom.

Historians surmise that over thirty years, thousands of slaves found their way to freedom via Guilford County's Quaker settlement. Although Coffin moved on, first to Indiana and later to Ohio, he was one of the key people responsible for organizing the Underground Railroad.

False Bottom to True Freedom

Quakers in North Carolina supported the abolitionist movement, but did so without violent acts. Richard Mendenhall, a Quaker who lived in Jamestown in the High Point area, hid slaves in a wagon with a false bottom, and transported many to freedom. You can still see the wagon he used and his home at Mendenhall Plantation in High Point.

N★C CIVIL WAR TRIVIA

Q. What battlefield was the site of the largest and bloodiest battle in North Carolina? (Hint: it's in Johnston County.)

A. Bentonville Battlefield.

Q. What percent of Southern casualties in the Civil War were North Carolinians?

A. An amazing 25 percent of all Southern Civil War casualties were North Carolinians.

Q. During the Civil War, nearly four hundred successful blockade runners obtained supplies for North Carolina by sailing to what port?

A. Nassau, Bahamas.

Q. What Fayetteville native was said to be the best blockade runner of them all?

A. J. N. Maffitt.

Q. How were Union troops occupying the grounds of the state capitol building in Raleigh informed that the war was over?

A. A signal, a kind of flare, was fired from the roof of the capitol building.

Q. What was the difference in monthly pay between a Confederate brigadier general and a Union one?

A. Fourteen dollars—Confederate generals earned $301 and Union generals $315.

Q. Where can you find the remains of the Confederate ram, the *Albemarle*, on display?

A. At the Port-O-Plymouth Civil War Museum in Plymouth.

Q. What fort was part of the Cape Fear line of defense and fell to Union soldiers in February 1865, allowing Wilmington to come under Union control?

A. Fort Anderson, nearly 90 percent intact and now a state historic site.

Q. What historical home in Hillsborough once served as headquarters for Confederate General Wade Hampton and is where General Joseph E. Johnston drafted the surrender papers he later gave to General William T. Sherman in April 1865?

A. Alexander Dickson House.

Q. What was the name of the battle over the Dismal Swamp Canal?

A. The Battle of South Mills.

Q. Where was the first Freedmen's Colony established in America?

A. Manteo.

Q. Where was the first Provisional Government of the Civil War established?

A. Hatteras.

Q. Who was the physician at the famous Confederate prison in Salisbury?

A. Josephus Hall.

Q. What Union general made Josephus Hall's home his headquarters in April 1865?

A. General George Stoneman. (The Josephus Hall House in Salisbury is still intact, with tours offered by costumed guides.)

10
Wheelers and Dealers

Playing "Chicken" in Valle Crucis

In 1883 a general store was established in Valle Crucis, and now Boone, Waynesville, Hendersonville, and Asheville have similar emporiums. This store's original motto was "Goods for the living, coffins and caskets for the dead." It was established by Henry Taylor, who became partners with W. W. Mast and later sold him all interests to the store. It's now known as Mast

At Mast General Store in Valle Crucis, you can see the original "chicken trapdoor" that was used to thwart pranksters. (PHOTO BY J. D. DOOLEY. USED WITH PERMISSION.)

General Store, and offers "everything you need for life in the nineteenth century and most of this one."

Around 1909, a man named Farthing owned another general store down the street. Both stores bartered for goods, often taking chickens in trade. Some local boys saw that Farthing put the chickens in a coop in his backyard. They came up with a devious plan, retrieving the chickens and taking them for trade, this time to Mast General Store.

No one knows how many times the same chickens were "rebartered," but Mast caught on to the trickery and installed a trapdoor inside his store. It led into the basement under the building, where the chickens were safe from youthful chicken recyclers. Next time you're in Valle Crucis, ask anyone at Mast General Store to show you the chicken trapdoor.

N★C Strange . . . but true

Why do people think of California instead of North Carolina when they think of the first gold rush in America? Photography didn't exist when gold was discovered in North Carolina—and debuted only four years before the California Gold Rush. So journalism and photography have left us a skewed sense of history when it comes to discovering gold.

All That Glitters . . . Makes a Good Doorstop

It was a beautiful day in the spring of 1799, and young Conrad Reed very much wanted to make a foray to the creek on his family's farm in Stanfield. "Please, Pa," he probably begged his German-born father, John Reed. It was Sunday, and Reed probably hesitated before allowing his young son some time to relax in the sun. Finally, he relented, and off young Conrad went with his siblings, who also were allowed to skip church that day.

Conrad wandered the woods on the Reed Farm in Cabarrus County, before coming to Little Meadow Creek. Near the creek banks, something yellow glinted in the water. Curious, Conrad took the seventeen-pound rock home to show his father.

Young Conrad Reed's discovery of a gleaming, yellow rock in Little Meadow Creek led to America's first gold rush. (PEN AND INK BY BUCK O'DONNELL. COURTESY REED GOLD MINE STATE HISTORIC SITE.)

John Reed, most likely born in Germany as Johannes Reith, had been a Hessian soldier who had left the ranks of the British Army at the end of the Revolutionary War. He had settled in Cabarrus County to be near his fellow Germans. Like most farmers in those days, Reed was semi-literate at best, and consumed by practical matters such as his corn and wheat crops. The family decided that the rock would make a good doorstop, and there it sat on the floor, propping open a door, for three years.

As time went on, John Reed became curious about the yellow stone, and in 1802 he took it to a jeweler in Fayetteville. The jeweler, amazed to see a seventeen-pound stone of solid gold right there on his countertop, sensed that the farmer didn't know much about the price of the precious metal. "How much do you want for it?" he asked.

Reed paused for a moment. It had been a good doorstop, but here was someone asking to buy it from him. He asked what he thought was a huge amount in those times—three dollars and fifty cents.

John Reed had just sold the first piece of gold ever documented to be discovered in the United States—and it had a value of about $3,600. As word got out about gold in the lower Piedmont area, Reed must have realized his naïveté with the jeweler, and started learning what he could about the creek-mining process. The next year, he formed a partnership called Reed Gold

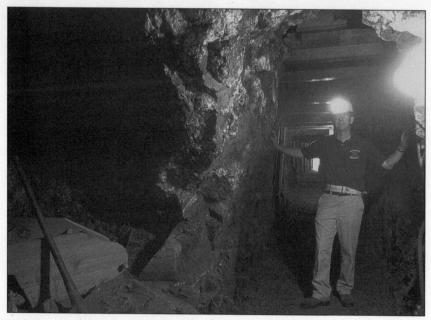

A visitor explores the tunnels at Reed Gold Mine in Stanfield. (COURTESY N.C. DIVISION OF TOURISM, FILM, AND SPORTS DEVELOPMENT)

Mine with men he knew and trusted: Frederick Kiser, Reverend James Love, and Martin Phifer Jr.

They continued with their farming and mined in the off-season, when the waters in the creek were at their lowest and the creek bed easiest to mine. The first year, Peter, one of Reed's slaves, discovered the biggest single nugget, weighing a whopping twenty-eight pounds.

Gold fever spread, and other people living in the Piedmont area explored their creekbeds with pans and rockers. News of the gold discoveries went out around the world, attracting English miners. When in 1825 gold was also found in veins of white quartz rock, an interest in underground gold mining increased. Mining this way was much more expensive, and Reed and his partners didn't start underground mining until 1831.

But there was soon to be trouble in Paradise, even among the nouveau riche Reeds. A family quarrel broke out concerning the mine business, resulting in a court injunction that closed the mine for ten long years. After John Reed died a wealthy man in 1845, the mine was sold at public auction. It changed hands several times, but during the California Gold Rush of 1849 the mine fell into disuse.

Now in the hands of the state of North Carolina, the Reed Gold Mine is open to tourists who want to try their hand at panning for gold. The establishment also shows films highlighting the first gold discovery and tours of restored portions of the underground mining tunnels. The Reed Gold Mine has found a new kind of gold these days—tourism.

Did You Know? The Tarheel State is a geologist's and rockhound's dream. North Carolina is the only state that has produced all four of the major gemstones—diamonds, emeralds, rubies, and sapphires. In addition, more than three hundred different minerals have been found in North Carolina. Mines throughout the state will let you try your luck at gem mining. Castle McCulloch in Jamestown is a restored gold refinery listed on the National Register of Historic Places, circa 1832, and this sure-enough castle (complete with stone walls three feet thick, a drawbridge, and a seventy-foot tower) offers tours and gem panning. A gold mill and museum are also on the premises, and it's such a picturesque venue that some people have their weddings and receptions there.

Castle McCulloch in Jamestown, a restored gold refinery, offers tours and gem panning. (COURTESY CASTLE MCCULLOCH. PHOTO BY BG PHOTOGRAPHY.)

Gatling and His "Lifesaving" Gun

Born in Maney's Neck, Hertford County, Richard Gatling was a plantation owner's son who began fiddling around with farm machinery as a young boy. His interest in making machinery to increase efficiency on his father's farm led the young man to invent a cottonseed-sowing machine, a machine to thin cotton plants in the field, a screw propeller, and a rice-sowing machine, among others.

He was traveling by boat to Philadelphia when the boat became icebound; Gatling was stricken with smallpox, with no physician on board to care for him. After this trip, the industrious Gatling enrolled in medical school in Cincinnati, Ohio, so he would never again be helpless in a medical crisis.

After inventing a hemp-processing machine and a steam plow, Gatling turned his attention to military machines and invented a steam ram to be used by warships. Then he began thinking back to the rapid-sowing machines he had invented and thought, why not invent a similar machine—one that fired bullets?

Dr. Richard Gatling hoped that his rapid-firing gun would save lives by replacing hundreds of people on the battlefield. (COURTESY N.C. DEPT. OF CULTURAL RESOURCES)

The man who had taken the Hippocratic oath in Ohio had noble intentions in inventing such a weapon. A rapid-firing gun, he reasoned, could replace hundreds of people on the battlefield, thereby saving lives. It could eliminate the need for large armies, and therefore large numbers of casualties.

On November 4, 1862, Gatling was awarded patent number 36,836 for his rapid-fire gun equipped with six rifle barrels, shooting approximately two hundred bullets a minute. Although one general used twelve of the guns in the James River campaign of May and June 1864 in the Civil War, he did so without proper military authorization. With typical government bureaucratic speed, by the time authorization was given for use, the war was over.

The Gatling Gun was further modified to ten barrels shooting three hundred shots per minute. It was used around the world in the Spanish-American War, the Franco-Prussian War, and the Russo-Japanese War.

Ironically, the gun invented by a man sworn to save lives, a gun developed to stop wars and mass human destruction, only expanded upon that theme.

Did You Know? The world's largest Duncan Phyfe chair is in Thomasville, built to acknowledge the large number of chairs made in the town's factories. The original chairs were pine, but this one is steel and concrete, set in a twelve-foot limestone base, and eighteen feet tall.

Making the Headlines: Josephus Daniels

Born in May 1862 in Washington, North Carolina, Josephus Daniels was the son of a Confederate shipbuilder. He lost his father before he was even a toddler, and his mother, Mary, struggled to make ends meet to provide for Josephus and his two brothers. Eventually the family moved to Wilson, where Mary became postmistress, and young Daniels found the calling for his life's work.

Josephus held down several odd jobs to help with the family income, but what intrigued him the most was working in a printing office. He became fascinated with newspaper publishing. At age sixteen, Josephus owned a newspaper, the *Cornucopia,* with his brother Charles, and Josephus edited another publication, *Our Free Blade.* By age eighteen, he bought out all interests supporting the newspaper, the *Advance,* covering four counties, and used the periodical as a platform to hold forth on political issues dear to his heart, such as temperance and trade.

In 1882 the brothers established the *Free Press* in Kinston. The young newspaper magnate campaigned for the Democratic Party and Grover Cleveland, using his latest newspaper as the pulpit for his editorial sermons. All this before entering college!

Daniels attended Wilson Collegiate Institute, then studied law in 1885 at the University of North Carolina at Chapel Hill and passed the bar the same year. Although he never practiced law, he combined his legal acumen with his business sense to purchase two newspapers in Raleigh, the *State Chronicle* and the *Farmer and Mechanic,* and merged them into one. The new *State Chronicle* served Daniels as a platform for his own politics, and he was elected printer to the state, an office he held from 1887 through 1893.

Buying and selling newspapers as suited his business and political interests, Daniels served in Washington, D.C., in the Department of the Interior. In 1894 he returned to Raleigh after purchasing the Raleigh-based newspaper, *News & Observer.*

Outspoken and inflammatory in his beliefs, Daniels held forth on topics ranging from Jim Crow laws, trusts, Southern railroad companies that ran politics in the South, and sensationalized crimes. Although his newspaper was given the derogatory nickname "Nuisance and Disturber," Daniels's belief that dullness was an editorial crime helped his newspaper to become the first in the world to have more subscribers than the population of the city in which it was headquartered. Even William Randolph Hearst offered to buy the *News & Observer* (he was turned down).

In 1912 Daniels promoted Woodrow Wilson for president of the United States, and Wilson then appointed Daniels secretary of the navy, a position he held from 1912 to 1921. Daniels, in turn, appointed a young man as his assistant secretary—Franklin Delano Roosevelt.

In 1932, although Daniels was encouraged to run for state governor, he turned his attention to promoting Roosevelt for the presidency. When Roosevelt won the office, Daniels was named ambassador to Mexico.

His years there were tumultuous: the American Embassy was stoned upon his arrival because the people blamed Daniels for the bad luck they had experienced for nearly two decades. Under President Wilson, when Daniels was secretary of the navy, the navy had bombarded the Mexican Naval Academy at Vera Cruz, then invaded Mexico and ousted its president, General Victoriano Huerta. These among other things were blamed on the fiery-penned newspaperman.

Despite this, Daniels worked to improve relations between Mexico and the United States, and during his tenure supported a plan for universal education in Mexico.

In 1941 his wife, Addie, became ill, and Daniels resigned and resumed his leadership at the newspaper, continuing his anything-but-dull editorial tradition. After his wife's death, the government commissioned the SS *Addie Daniels* in her honor in 1944.

Daniels penned four books about his military experiences, two relating to the navy and two on Woodrow Wilson. Daniels died in January 1948, but the *News & Observer* made him immortal—and a middle school in Raleigh bears his name today.

Did You Know? Calling coffee a "cup of Joe" started as a naval term. When Josephus Daniels was secretary of the navy, among other changes, he eliminated intoxicants aboard naval ships. Legend says that sailors began drinking more coffee because of "Joe's" alcohol ban.

The Rub That Relieved Millions

In the 1890s a young pharmacist in Greensboro named Lunsford Richardson found himself facing the dilemma so many parents faced then: his son Smith had the croup, and anything used as a poultice irritated his baby's skin. What could he do?

Richardson decided to ask his brother-in-law to use his laboratory to do some experiments. The pharmacist finally hit on a mixture of a Japanese mint oil (menthol), camphor, and eucalyptus in a base of petroleum jelly, and found that it gave relief to croupy coughs. Body heat caused the rub to vaporize, and through inhalation and absorption of the medicines in the petroleum jelly, the patient found relief.

Successfully selling the rub locally, by 1905 Richardson invested his entire life savings in a laboratory, and his son went to work with him. They changed the name of the rub from Richardson's Croup and Pneumonia Cure Salve to honor the brother-in-law who had loaned his laboratory, and set about on the first mass-mailing campaign in the United States. The salve was an instant hit both in the states and internationally, and Richardson died in 1919 a wealthy man.

The brother-in-law's name was Dr. Joshua Vick. And the salve? You know it today as Vick's VapoRub.

The "Rose Buddies" of Elizabeth City

About twenty years ago, Elizabeth City had little to attract tourists to its small, quaint, and friendly town. The village seemed to be in need of something that would make it more than just a quiet town on the shores of the Pasquotank River in northeastern North Carolina.

Two long-time residents and friends, Fred Fearing and Joe Kramer, met after church one Sunday and discovered more than a dozen visiting yachtsmen docking at the newly completed Mariners' Wharf. The Pasquotank flows into the Atlantic Ocean, and the city had just finished building a wharf that allowed sailors a complimentary forty-eight-hour dockage.

Being of a social bent, the two Southern gentlemen serendipitously decided to throw a party for the wharf's first visitors, thinking it would be a nice way to say thank you. They rounded up wine, cheese, and all the accompaniments. Kramer went to his rose garden and clipped seventy roses for the wives, or "first mates," of these initial visiting sailors. From this first modest reception, something phenomenal resulted.

Inspired by the two self-made marketing men, the town hosts a reception every evening, April through November, for sailors visiting the waterfront city. On any of those nights, if you sail into port and dock at Mariners' Wharf you will be treated like a visiting dignitary. In 1981 Joe Kramer passed away, but his roses were transplanted to Mariners' Wharf and continue to bloom there. Meanwhile, Fred Fearing has taken over the clipping and giving of the roses. At a certain time of year, he hands out something else. "When the weather gets too cool for roses, and the cotton is ready, I hand the ladies cotton bolls and tell them, 'Now you're a cotton-picking North Carolinian,'" says Fearing.

Elizabeth City and its growing number of "rose buddies" have become internationally famous for their hospitality to the boating community. Such

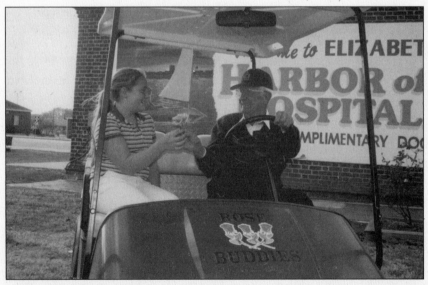

Fred Fearing, one of the original "Rose Buddies," hands a rose to visitor Sarah Lacey. The people of Elizabeth City welcome visiting sailors with a fee-free pier and a reception, boosting the economy of this quaint town. (PHOTO BY THE AUTHOR)

notables as Walter Cronkite, Bill Friday (former president of the University of North Carolina), and NBC personality Willard Scott have been guests. Scott also gave the town its first "rose buddies" golf cart. You will often see Fearing in it, greeting newcomers who arrive by sea looking for a welcoming port. And they discover it in Elizabeth City—more bustling than it used to be, but still just as friendly and charming.

The Birthplace of Pepsi-Cola

In New Bern in the 1890s, a young pharmacist named Caleb Bradham kept experimenting with kola and coca extracts, trying to hit on a drink that would taste good and make people feel good, too. The young man affectionately known as "Doc" finally made the perfect concoction of sweeteners, flavorings, and carbonated water. Friends raved about the new soda and dubbed it "Brad's Drink," but Bradham kept looking for a name with more "oomph" to it. He found out about a registered name that was for sale by a New Jersey company and bought the rights to the name "Pep Kola" for a hundred dollars. This became Pepsi-Cola, and within ten years Doc Bradham was a rich man, with the soda marketed in twenty-four states.

After World War I was declared, however, financial problems hit. Bradham had invested nearly everything he had in sugar stocks, thinking the price would go up because of the war. It dropped instead, and he declared bankruptcy in 1923.

After being owned by several holding companies, the Pepsi formula was bought by the Loft Candy Company of New York. Now there are more than seven hundred bottling facilities around the world.

Bradham's two drugstores still stand in New Bern. His first is on the corner of Pollock and Middle Streets with a banner that reads, "The Birthplace of Pepsi-Cola." The second, at the corner of Broad and Middle streets, has been renovated into a wonderful eatery called the Chelsea Restaurant. Although the rest of the building has been altered to serve the needs of restaurant patrons, the downstairs has kept the look and feel of Doc Bradham's turn-of-the-century drugstore, complete with pressed tin ceiling and mosaic tile floor.

Did You Know? You can still see a bit of the legendary "Land of Oz" in North Carolina. Developers built a theme park, the Land of Oz, based on L. Frank Baum's book *The Wonderful Wizard of Oz*, on Beech Mountain in Watauga County. The park thrived in the late 1960s and 1970s, but closed in 1980. You can still see many items from the park on display in the Appalachian Cultural Museum at Appalachian State University in Boone.

The "Hole" Truth about Krispy Kreme

Winston-Salem is the home of the world-famous Krispy Kreme Doughnuts, established in 1937 by Vernon Rudolph. While Rudolph was operating a doughnut shop in Paducah, Kentucky, he got the now-famous doughnut recipe from a French chef from New Orleans. Taking the recipe with him, Rudolph set up shop in Winston-Salem.

The rest is entrepreneurial history: Krispy Kreme now produces collectively more than two billion doughnuts a day, with shops making anywhere from three thousand to twelve thousand doughnuts per hour (depending on the size of the shop). But there's more to the story than just numbers.

Krispy Kreme has developed a kind of following, and the doughnut that gave coffee the best break it ever had is a part of Southern culture. Shops have opened as far away as Los Angeles and New York City, and the Krispy Kreme phenomenon has been discussed on National Public Radio. There's a Krispy Kreme website (www.krispykreme.com), on which you can sign up to become a member of "Friends of Krispy Kreme." Since *InStyle Magazine* mentioned Krispy Kreme doughnuts in their wedding issue (Spring 2002), wedding planners by the thousands have been calling their local doughnut shops, ordering doughnuts for receptions. Krispy Kreme is such a part of the culture, that when area residents in Raleigh petitioned the courts to have a local Krispy Kreme shop's sign made smaller and less gaudy, the doughnut company won the decision in court to keep the sign, and now the shop's sign at 549 Person Street has landmark status.

Hey, after all, it's not just a doughnut—it's the epitome of the American dream. Glazed.

Lost and Found: The Queen Anne's Revenge

The ship once sailed by Blackbeard may rejuvenate the area of North Carolina that the infamous pirate terrorized during his years of piracy. The *Queen Anne's Revenge* had been in the waters of the Atlantic since she ran aground in 1718. Then in November 1996, Intersal Incorporated, a Florida-based diving and treasure-hunting company, found the wreckage in only twenty-five feet of water in Beaufort Inlet. Recovered items include a bronze bell from 1709, a cannonball weighing twenty-four pounds, and a sounding weight.

As artifacts from the *Queen Anne's Revenge* continue to be discovered in what are now protected waters, interest in the ship and its historical context have increased exponentially. The artifacts are on display at the North Carolina Maritime Museum in Beaufort, and twice a year, the *Queen Anne's Revenge* Project in cooperation with the museum holds an interactive dive called "DiveLive" for schoolchildren and other interested persons. In 2002 the Maritime Museum opened a repository for the *Queen Anne's Revenge* artifacts, with interactive displays, a diorama of the wreck site, a model of the ship, and more. The repository is about a mile from the museum on West Beaufort Road near the airport.

It seems that after nearly three hundred years, the people of North Carolina may now be getting some of Blackbeard's treasure—in the form of scientific research, government grants, and tourist dollars.

Did You Know? In Beaufort you can see a house said to have once been a tavern used by Blackbeard and his crew. It's now a private dwelling named Hammock House.

The Dukes of Durham

At the end of the Civil War, Washington Duke returned to his wife and three sons at their home in Durham and discovered that virtually everything of value had been taken or destroyed. One twenty-five-pound sack of raw tobacco leaves, however, had not been discovered in its hiding place.

Duke and his sons prepared the leaves and sold them for a surprisingly good price, as during the war soldiers on both sides had come to enjoy what they called "bright leaf" tobacco. (Today, virtually all coastal-plain tobacco is the bright leaf, flue-cured variety, which is used nearly exclusively for cigarettes.) From this nest egg, Duke became a tobacco manufacturer and started a factory that prepared tobacco for market, called W. Duke & Sons Tobacco Company.

The living they made was adequate but modest. Then in 1884 Duke heard of a machine that would roll cigarettes, invented by James Bonsack of Virginia. Immediately, he bought the patent rights for what others dismissed as a machine that probably wouldn't be profitable. Before long, Duke's

Washington Duke stands next to his first tobacco factory, which was actually a converted corncrib. Fifteen thousand pounds of smoking tobacco was produced in one year using this building. (COURTESY DUKE HOMESTEAD STATE HISTORIC SITE, DURHAM, N.C.)

tobacco company had something akin to a world-wide monopoly in the cigarette industry, and Durham became the tobacco capital of the world.

By 1907 the Duke tobacco estate was worth more than $300 million, and in 1924 Washington's son, Buck, decided to be philanthropic with some of the profits. He created a world-class university from the former Trinity College (previously moved to Durham), which was renamed Duke University that same year. Buck Duke then added more buildings, dormitories, and the magnificent Duke Chapel, surrounded by 20,000 lush acres.

At the Duke Homestead State Historic Site and Tobacco Museum, you can see where Washington Duke first came home to bad news—and learn how one family took "lemons" and made their own version of lemonade.

N★C Strange . . . but true

An Accident That Led to a Billion-Dollar Industry

The method used for curing cigarette tobacco was developed by accident, according to Sallie Anderson, Caswell County historian. In 1839, deep into the tobacco-harvesting season of that fall, Stephen Slade, a slave owned by Abishai Slade, was left to monitor the barn full of tobacco as it cured overnight. In those days farmers cured tobacco by hanging it in the barn, leaving a four-foot space between the tobacco and the floor. The floor was then spread with hot charcoals, which had to be replenished to maintain a constant temperature. That night the sentinel, Stephen Slade, fell asleep, waking to find the coals nearly out. He hurried to the blacksmith's forge nearby and brought back fresh, hot coals for the floor. It turned out that lowering the heat, and then raising it again, caused the tobacco to improve in flavor and color. The Museum in Yanceyville has a letter, addressed to Abishai Slade from tobacco buyers in Richmond, on the exceptional quality of the tobacco he produced from then on.

Sunken Treasure, Avast!

Near the town of Wilmington is a small fishing village called Carolina Beach, settled by a family whose last name was Winner. Their descendant, Captain Carl "Skippy" Winner, lives up to his family name—he's a diver who searches sunken ocean-going crafts for salvage. Winner has discovered sunken treasure, but not gems or gold: he makes a living salvaging wrecks and selling what he finds. For fifty years, Winner has been diving on blockade runners, looking for salvageable artifacts. Some of the artifacts he has recovered are on display at the Smithsonian in Washington, D.C.; the Naval Museum in Newport News, Virginia; and the North Carolina Museum of History in Raleigh.

Carolina Beach has an easygoing ambience that belies its history: this area has been more than once fraught with violence, as desperate soldiers and civilians alike found themselves caught up in the Civil War, and generations later, World War II. The ports in the area were some of the last open to the Confederacy, explains Winner, and were used by increasingly desperate blockade runners transporting goods to civilians and soldiers—and many

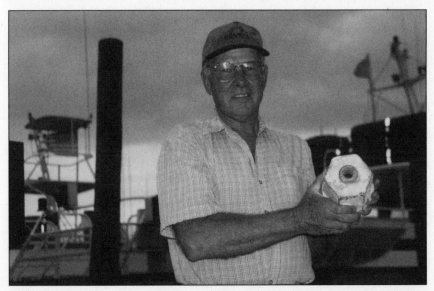

Captain Skippy Winner stands aboard one of his boats, holding a bronze lug nut he dove for and salvaged from a sunken wreck—it may not look like treasure, but for him it is.
(PHOTO BY THE AUTHOR)

met their fate in these waters. (You can read more about blockade runners in Chapter 9.) Similarly, German U-boats made quite a few attempts to invade the United States via these same small ports. Many met the same fate as the blockade runners, and now lie on the ocean floor.

Winner became fascinated early on by the history that lies beneath the waves. As a teenager, he began diving the waters near his home, with a diving regulator he made himself. Realizing that much could be recovered from the ocean floor, he began salvaging in 1956 and eventually built up a salvage operation with a fleet of nine boats.

His fascination with history led him to read about the Civil War blockade runners and World War II German U-boats in the area. "You can look out over the waters around here," Winner says, "and at low tide, see the top of sunken blockade runners' ships." An underwater-salvager is a combination of historian, detective, and diver, Winner explains. He researches each wreck intensely, finding out details of the ship and its sinking, and the lay of the ocean floor.

One of his biggest salvage operations was in nine fathoms of water twenty-seven miles off the Masonboro Inlet, where a tanker named the *John D. Gill* was hit by a German torpedo and sunk. It had been under water since 1941, but despite time, tides, waves, and a ten-foot tiger shark the divers named George, Winner and his crew salvaged much of the ship. The salvage job paid forty-nine cents a pound—in one year, Winner salvaged 190,000 pounds of brass, 17,000 pounds of copper, and 8,000 pounds of copper-nickel (you do the math!). Not a bad living at all, it seems, reaping the sunken treasure just beneath the waves.

Winner will take you out to sea if you want to try your hand at finding valuable artifacts. Who knows what you may find? Here are just a few samples of Winner's sunken "treasures:"

★ Prehistoric clam shells, oyster shells, and animal bones

★ Foreign coins

★ An anchor chain from a Spanish galleon

★ Civil War–era bullets, knives, guns, shoes, and china

★ A World War II–era cannon

★ Human remains from a World War II German U-boat

★ Porcelain toilets ("nothing grows on porcelain and they are a beautiful sight")

★ A completely made bunk bed and a wooden footlocker full of clothes from the American World War II tanker *John D. Gill*

N★C WHEELERS AND DEALERS TRIVIA

Q. What was the name of R. J. and Katherine Reynolds's home, located outside Winston-Salem?

A. Reynolda. It is now used as an art museum.

Q. Before the Civil War, what city in North Carolina was the site of a U.S. mint?

A. Charlotte.

Q. What town on the Pasquotank River gets its name from its main business of building small commercial sea-going vessels?

A. Shipyard.

Q. What does the seated figure on the North Carolina State Seal symbolize?

A. Plenty.

Q. What town has a museum called Mill Village Museum, depicting life in a company-owned mill town?

A. Cooleemee, Davie County.

Q. Where is the famous blacksmith shop owned by Mike and Bea Hensley, artisans who have created works for the Smithsonian and for well-known people?

A. Spruce Pine.

Q. What town in North Carolina manufactures the most denim in the world?

A. Erwin.

Q. In what city in North Carolina can you attend the world's largest furniture show?

A. High Point.

Q. By what produce is the town of Mount Olive known (it's not olives!)?

A. Its nickname is "Pickle Town, USA."

Q. What is the *Fayetteville Observer*'s claim to fame?

A. It is North Carolina's oldest newspaper; it began publishing in 1816.

Q. Where can you find a museum featuring the history of the Carolina Freight Company and the story of its founder, C. Grier Beam?

A. In Cherryville. The museum is named the C. Grier Beam Truck Museum.

Q. What artist and furniture crafter helped put the town of Lexington on the map?

A. Bob Timberlake.

Q. What town is famous for its hand-crafted pottery?

A. Seagrove.

Q. Where was the first Hardee's Hamburgers established, and in what year?

A. In Rocky Mount, 1960.

Q. What is the name of the town that, complete with a rodeo, saloon, marshal, horses-only Main Street, and dance hall, was established as the East's only Western town?

A. Love Valley.

11
Film, Music, and Drama

Hollywood in North Carolina

After New York and California, more movies, documentaries, and TV shows are filmed in North Carolina than any other state. Since 1980, more than five hundred movies, several thousand commercials, and more than a half-dozen TV series have used the Tarheel State as their setting. The state has been so popular for moviemaking that Wilmington is home to Screen Gems Studio, whose president is Frank Capra Jr. Outside Hollywood, there's no larger full-service studio and sound stage production facility. North Carolina also has a half-dozen other production facilities, offering twenty-seven sound stages in addition to those at Screen Gems. One noteworthy studio is Hollywood East in Shelby, with the largest cyclorama stage in the world.

The camera rolls in Wilmington as Jodie Foster plays her role in The Dangerous Lives of Altar Boys. (Courtesy N.C. Film Commission)

Why has North Carolina become the eastern version of Hollywood?

Callie Khouri directs the filming of the Divine Secrets of the Ya-Ya Sisterhood *in Wilmington.* (COURTESY N.C. FILM COMMISSION)

Climate is a draw, as is the scenic and geographical diversity—not to mention the friendly people.

Here's just a sample of the hundreds of films made in North Carolina:

★ *The Color Purple* (1985)

★ *Bull Durham* (1988)

 ★ *A Stoning in Fulham County* (1988)

★ *The Ryan White Story* (1989)

★ *Days of Thunder* (1990)

★ *The Last of the Mohicans* (1992)

★ *The Fugitive* (1993)

★ *Nell* (1994)

★ *Richie Rich* (1994)

★ *Patch Adams* (1998)

★ *The Rage: Carrie 2* (1999)

★ *The Original Kings of Comedy* (2000)

★ *Black Knight* (2001)

★ *Domestic Disturbance* (2001)

★ *Hannibal* (2001)

★ *Shallow Hal* (2001)

★ *Divine Secrets of the Ya-Ya Sisterhood* (2002)

★ *A Walk to Remember* (2002)

Hurrah! The Old North State Forever!

William Gaston wrote "The Old North State" (the town of Gastonia was named after him) and Mrs. E. E. Rudolph collected and arranged the music. In 1927 the General Assembly officially adopted this as the state song of North Carolina. Here are the words, so you can sing along!

The Old North State

Carolina! Carolina! Heaven's blessings attend her!
While we live we will cherish, protect, and defend her;
Tho' the scorner may sneer at and witlings defame her,
Still our hearts swell with gladness whenever we name her.
(Chorus): Hurrah! Hurrah! The Old North State forever!
Hurrah! Hurrah! the good Old North State!

Tho' she envies not others, their merited glory,
Say whose name stands the foremost, in liberty's story,
Tho' too true to herself e'er to crouch to oppression,
Who can yield to just rule a more loyal submission.
(Repeat chorus)

Then let all those who love us, love the land that we live in,
As happy a region as on this side of heaven,
Where plenty and peace, love and joy smile before us,
Raise aloud, raise together the heart thrilling chorus.
(Repeat chorus)

The Story of the "Songcatcher"

In 1908 a woman named Olive Dame Campbell accompanied her minister husband to the Appalachian Mountains. His work was to save souls, and she became a "songcatcher," a term used to describe someone who collects songs.

Stunned by the beauty of the mountaineers' songs and their talents when it came to crafts, Campbell began collecting the ancient ballads and studying and recording how handcrafts were made. In 1925 she founded the John C. Campbell Folk School in Brasstown, named for her husband and established to record and teach traditional Appalachian Mountain ways. What the "songcatcher" began is now the oldest folk school in the United States, and offers classes in mountain musical and craft traditions.

Did You Know? In 1928 Benny Davis was inspired by the view from the bridge and causeway on the Perquimans River in Hertford to write the song "Carolina Moon." Incidentally, that bridge is the only S-shaped drawbridge in the world.

"Tweet" Success

If you think you're any good at the art of whistling—or just want to see what is perhaps the largest gathering of such musicians—then check out Louisburg's Annual International Whistling Competition, held every April. As part of the Whistlers' Convention, the competition requires each contestant to whistle one classical tune and a tune from a pop song.

So the winners of the competition aren't just whistling Dixie.

Mary Frances Herndon performs her art at the International Whistlers Competiton in Louisburg. (COURTESY GEORGE MANLEY AND THE FRANKLIN COUNTY ARTS COUNCIL)

The Song of the "Chanteymen"

In the coastal area around Beaufort as late as the 1940s and 1950s, a group of local African American fishermen sang as they plied their trade in the waters. These were traditional work songs that went back generations. "The songs were sung so that all the men pulling on the nets would be in synchronicity," Connie Mason, Beaufort historian, explains, and these fishermen were called the Chanteymen. Unfortunately, mechanization brought an end to the Chanteymen in the 1950s when hydraulic blocks were used to pull up nets, eliminating the need for large crews to haul the nets.

Although the era of the singing fishermen is past, the songs of the Chanteymen have been preserved in recordings in the North Carolina Maritime Museum in Beaufort. Here are the words to a few stanzas of one such song, author unknown, provided by Connie Mason.

I'm Gonna Roll Here

I'm gonna roll here / Roll here a few days longer (pull)
I'm gonna roll here / Roll here a few days longer (pull)
Then I'm going home, boys / Lord, Lord, I'm going home (pull)
I left my baby / Standing in the back door crying (pull)
I left my baby / Standing in the back door crying (pull)
Saying, Daddy don't you go / Lord, Lord, Daddy don't you go (pull)

"Saint" John Coltrane

Acknowledged as one of the more prolific as well as versatile players in jazz, John William Coltrane has left a legacy that transcends the world of music. He died in 1967, but his life and music continue to shape the lives of others.

Coltrane was born in 1926 in the town of Hamlet to John R. and Alice Blair Coltrane. His father was a tailor but also an amateur musician, and his grandfather a presiding elder in the African Methodist Episcopal Zion Church in High Point, where Coltrane was raised.

When Coltrane was still a young boy, his father, grandparents, and an uncle died, leaving his mother obliged to find work as a domestic to support herself and her son.

Coltrane played first the clarinet and horn, then the alto saxophone when he joined the high school band. After he graduated from high school, the family moved to Philadelphia, where the young sax player began playing in local clubs. In 1945, when he was drafted into the navy and stationed in Hawaii, Coltrane played with other sailor-musicians, and in 1946 he made his first release, with singer Tadd Dameron (*Hot House,* Rhino Records).

Once out of the navy, Coltrane moved back to Philadelphia, switched from alto to tenor sax, and played with several bands. The high point was playing with Dizzy Gillespie, and his first solo during a performance of "We Love to Boogie."

That was in 1951. Coltrane had fallen victim to a heroin habit, and his addiction made him unreliable. Coltrane was fired by Johnny Hodges and then hired by Miles Davis, a former drug addict himself. Davis apparently saw the promise and potential in Coltrane's style, and worked to help the saxophone player kick the heroin habit.

Coltrane's performance at the Newport Jazz Festival in 1955 resulted in a recording contract with Columbia Records, and the New Miles Davis Quintet debuted with Prestige Records in 1956 before coming out with "Round About Midnight" for Columbia in 1957. Davis and Coltrane played together until April 1957, when Davis fired Coltrane because of his persistent heroin problem. Being fired may have been a wake-up call for Coltrane, who finally succeeded in kicking the heroin habit for good.

Coltrane played and recorded with Lee Morgan, Kenny Drew, and fellow North Carolinian Thelonius Monk, among others. His style became increasingly radical and experimental, and he became known not only for his prolific recordings (seven different labels carry his work), but also his commitment to jazz. One of his biggest commercial hits was his adaptation of Rodgers and Hammerstein's "My Favorite Things," the improvisation for which he is probably best known.

Coltrane's light was too soon extinguished, however, when he died of liver cancer in 1967. Coltrane is still regarded as one of the most influential jazz musicians ever, and received many music awards. In 1992 he was posthumously awarded the Grammy Lifetime Achievement Award.

The city of Hamlet honors him with the annual John Coltrane Jazz Festival, but Coltrane's legacy transcends music—and state borders. In 1965, in a nightclub in San Francisco, a hairdresser named Franzo Wayne King heard Coltrane and remarked that the experience was "a baptism in sound . . . a very serious and earnest journey to seek out God." Following this musical "baptism," King founded the Saint John Coltrane African Orthodox Church in San Francisco, using music as a way of touching people's souls. Now known to the seventy-plus members as Bishop King, he leads his flock in three-hour church services that are influenced by Coltrane's music and are part worship and part jam session (like Coltrane, Bishop King also plays saxophone).

Coltrane once said he hoped to show people the "divine in a musical language that transcends words, to speak to their soul." Now, decades after his death, the North Carolina jazz great is helping people find God through music.

Did You Know? Belhaven native Eva Narcissus Boyd's job before making it big in the music business was baby-sitting—for none other than Carole King and Gerry Goffin. The New York–based singer-songwriters had cowritten a song. They asked Boyd, who had a good voice, to record it for them as a demo. The demo was so good, producer Don Kirshner released it as it was (Dimension Records). You may know Boyd best as "Little Eva." The song? Remember "The Locomotion"? There in fact wasn't a dance called the Locomotion, but after the song became a Number One hit in August 1962, Little Eva created the famous dance to go with the song. She now lives in Kinston and appears in oldies shows.

Matching

Match the musician or singer with the description.

Descriptions

1. Born in Harris in 1908, this musician was a pioneer of the three-finger style of banjo playing and influenced many early bluegrass players, including Don Reno, Earl Scruggs, and Homer "Pappy" Sherill.

2. This phenomenal flat-picker from Stoney Fork Township, blind since infancy, first learned to play the harmonica and banjo, then played "When the Roses Bloom in Dixieland" on a borrowed guitar. His father was so excited he helped him purchase his first guitar—a Stella for twelve dollars.

3. He was born the youngest of thirteen in Greensboro and grew up with a love of singing, but got his nickname from football playing. His first recorded song was "Knock Three Times" and his Number One hits included "Rub It In" and "Ruby Baby."

4. Married for a time to singer Carly Simon, this singer-songwriter was born in Boston in 1948 and moved with his family to the Chapel Hill area in 1951. One of his endearing songs is *You've Got a Friend*, and his bluesy style and smooth-as-honey voice still entertain us.

5. This woman was born in Raleigh and could really belt out a tune. She was best known for her rendition of "God Bless America" and is buried in Lake Placid, New York.

6. This country music singer from Tabor City, best known for his 1959 country music hit "Waterloo," has a nickname that goes back to the Civil War.

7. Born in 1944 in Robbinsville, this singer won the Country Music Association's Entertainer of the Year Award in 1977.

8. This bluegrass guitarist and bandleader was born in Cleveland, and his

1969-era band was named for him. He played with Lester Flatt and is perhaps best known for their banjo duet, "Theme from the Beverly Hillbillies."

9. Born in Wilmington in 1936, this country music singer-songwriter also has a band named for him. He is probably best known for "The Devil Went Down to Georgia."

10. This jazz pianist was born in 1917 in Rocky Mount and developed the style of music known as bebop.

11. This musician, born in 1940, became a famous singer and pianist, but started as a music and English teacher in Farmville. Her most well known songs are *Killing Me Softly with His Song*, *The First Time Ever I Saw Your Face*, and *Feel Like Makin' Love*.

Names

A. Arthel L. "Doc" Watson.

B. Snuffy Jenkins

C. James Taylor

D. Billy "Crash" Craddock

E. Stonewall Jackson

F. Kate Smith

G. Earl Scruggs, and the Earl Scruggs Review

H. Ronnie Milsap

I. Thelonious Monk

J. Charlie Daniels, and the Charlie Daniels Band

K. Roberta Flack

ANSWERS: 1B, 2A, 3D, 4C, 5F, 6E, 7H, 8G, 9J, 10I, 11K

Other Famous Music Folk Born in North Carolina

★ **Clyde Edric Barron Bernhardt:** blues trombonist, Gold Hill.

★ **Joseph Leonard "Joe" Bonner:** pianist and composer, Rocky Mount.

★ **Margie Bowes:** country singer, Roxboro.

★ **Carol Brice:** contralto, Sedalia.

★ **Alden ("Allen") Bunn:** blues guitarist, near Wilson.

★ **J. C. Burris:** harmonica player, King's Mountain.

★ **Shirley Caesar:** known as "Baby Shirley, the Gospel Singer," started with the Charity Singers, Durham.

★ **George Clinton:** R&B songwriter, singer, bandleader, Kannapolis.

★ **Floyd ("Dipper Boy") Council:** nicknamed "Devil's Daddy-in-Law," blues guitarist and mandolin player, Chapel Hill.

★ **Mary Cardwell Dawson,** opera director, Meridian.

★ **Donna Fargo:** country music singer, best known for *Happiest Girl in the Whole U.S.A.* and *Funny Face,* Mount Airy.

★ **"Blind Boy" Fuller** (born Fulton Allen): blues man, Wadesboro.

★ **Don Gibson:** singer, best known for hit song "Oh, Lonesome Me," Shelby.

★ **George Hamilton IV:** country singer, Winston-Salem.

★ **Willie "Bill" Harris:** guitarist, Nashville.

★ **Kay Kyser:** famous bandleader of the 1940s, Rocky Mount.

★ **Weston Wilbur Little:** singer and bass musician, Parmele.

★ **John D. Loudermilk:** country musician who had his own radio program at age eleven, Durham.

★ **Clyde McPhatter:** R&B singer, Durham.

★ **Charlie Poole:** bluegrass banjo picker, who played with the North Carolina Ramblers, Randolph County.

★ **Del Reeves:** country music singer, best known for "Be Quiet Mind" in 1961, Sparta.

★ **Woody Shaw:** trumpet player, Laurinburg.

★ **Nina Simone** (born Eunice Waymon): soul singer, pianist, arranger, Tryon.

★ **William "Billy" Taylor:** pianist, composer, educator and musical director, Greeneville.

Helping Musicians, Preserving Music

Outside the town of Hillsborough is an old farmhouse that has been converted into a recording studio and administrative offices. This quiet place is the result of a vision shared by Timothy and Denise Duffy. Their mission is to give a hand to musicians living in poverty, while preserving little-known yet unique music before it's gone forever.

The Duffys' organization is called Music Maker Relief Foundation, and benefits musicians whose style is rooted in a Southern musical tradition, are fifty-five or older, and earn less than $18,000 annually. It began in the 1980s, when Timothy began booking blues musicians from nearby Winston-Salem and Greensboro. From the proceeds he started a foundation to help musicians in dire need with the most basic of necessities—such as a pair of new shoes.

Now more than a hundred musical artists are being helped with food, shelter, medical care, and other basic needs. They have an average income of six thousand dollars a year, and some are as far away as Canada and California.

The Duffys also preserve these musicians' works. While Denise handles the administrative end, Timothy travels to meet with musicians. He has recorded musicians' work in tumbledown shacks and fields, as well as in the Hillsborough studio. Many of these musicians, most of whom have been making music for fifty years or more, have never had their music recorded. The Duffys are also working to make sure that the music of Chicago, Memphis, Nashville, and the Mississippi Delta are not forgotten. They are preserving time on an album.

If you ever drive by their farm in Hillsborough, roll down your windows and listen. You just might hear something you have never heard before, being recorded for posterity in the Duffy studio.

When Waynesville Goes International

Since 1984 the city of Waynesville has hosted a music and dance festival unlike anything else in the state. Every July the townspeople celebrate the heritage of music and dance with an international folk festival called Folkmoot (an old English term meaning "a gathering of the people"). The North Carolina Folk Festival brings in dancers from such far-flung places as Togo, the Czech Republic, Mongolia, Paraguay, and more. Not only is Folkmoot a celebration of international cultures, but also a cultural exchange. Dancers entertain in several surrounding counties during their

Dancers from Sicily perform at Folkmoot, an international folk festival in Waynesville.
(COURTESY FOLKMOOT USA)

visit and stay in hostel-like quarters in a refurbished school, the Folkmoot Friendship Center.

For ten days every July, the town of Waynesville does more than show-case dancers from the world over—the people there become international diplomats of sorts, in the mountains of the Tarheel State.

Did You Know? The North Carolina Symphony travels around the state to introduce school children to classical music through its Symphony Day initiative. Since the first Symphony Day in 1946, the symphony has visited and played for more than three million school children.

Libba Cotten: Upside-down Music

Libba (Elizabeth) Cotten was born in Chapel Hill around 1892, but her music didn't hit it big until she was past her sixtieth birthday. Mostly she played for family until she made her professional debut in 1959 with Mike Seeger at a concert in Pennsylvania. From then on, she was regarded as a professional folk artist. Her best-known song is "Freight Train," which she wrote when she was twelve and was first recorded by several other groups, including Peter, Paul, and Mary.

When Cotten was a little girl, she desperately wanted to learn to play a musical instrument. Her brother had a banjo, and when Cotten asked if she could try her hand at it, he said no, as most siblings would. But the little girl was determined.

When her brother left the house, Libba would sneak into his room, where he kept his banjo under the bed. The problem was that Libba was left-handed, and the banjo was strung for a right-handed player. She couldn't change the way the strings were, because her brother would know she'd gotten to the instrument—so she played it upside down. When in later years Libba bought a guitar, she couldn't play it or tune it until she reversed the strings and played the only way she knew.

The left-handed, two-fingered picking style of Libba Cotten worked—in 1972 she won the National Folk Association's Burl Ives Award for her life-long contribution to folk music. Her last album, *Elizabeth Cotten Live,* won a Grammy for best traditional folk music, two years before her death in 1987.

N★C Stran©e . . . but true

His Music Makes You "Paws"

Saxophone player and Chapel Hill resident Joe Procopio says he's the world's only musical composer who writes tunes solely for the entertainment of animals, specifically canaries, dogs, and cats. Procopio says his neighbor's cockatiel lets out delightful chirps when he plays his music, two octaves higher than most tunes for humans. One reviewer says the music resembles Barry Manilow's music. Procopio would be tail-wagging happy if a record company would "leash" onto his music and put out a CD just for pets.

A Flair for the Dramatic

North Carolina is awash with annual dramatic performances, many of which are performed outdoors. Here's a partial list of plays and where they are performed.

★ *The Amistad Saga* (Raleigh)

★ *Blackbeard's Reveng*e (Swansboro)

★ *Cape Fear Shakespeare Festival* (Wilmington)

★ *First for Freedom* (Halifax)

★ *From This Day Forward* (Valdese)

★ *Horn in the West* (Boone)

★ *The Legend of Tom Dooley* (Wilkesboro)

★ *The Liberty Cart: A Duplin Story* (Kenansville)

★ *Listen and Remember* (Waxhaw)

★ *The Lost Colony* (Roanoke Island)

★ *The Rising Splendor* (New Bern)

★ *Strike at the Wind* (Pembroke)

★ *The Sword of Peace* (Snow Camp)

★ *Unto These Hills* (Cherokee)

★ *Worthy Is the Lamb* (Swansboro)

"The Hills Are Alive . . ."

North Carolina hills and valleys are alive with the sound of young male voices, raised together in perfect harmony, as they carry on a centuries-old tradition of all-boy choirs.

In 1971 Bill Graham arrived in Durham to become full-time director of music at the local First Presbyterian Church. "We had sort of a large music ministry back then, with separate choirs for boys and girls," he says. Apparently, Graham's work with the choir was noticed, as people began to come to his church to ask to sing with the choirs. Someone suggested a community boys' choir.

It started with about a dozen of the church's best singers, called the Durham Boys' Choir. Seemingly overnight, the choir grew to more than forty boys. "We didn't even guess the scope of what the choir would become," Graham says. "And someone told us that if we could last five years we'd be really doing something, and by then we should go on the road."

By 1975 Ben Smith, choral director at Duke University, called with a proposal. Duke was planning a Noah's Ark production that required three singing sons of Noah and forty-two singing animals. The problem was, it was spring, and school was almost out. Then one of the mothers suggested a week of camp for the choir, while the boys did the play.

After the three performances, suddenly the Durham Boys' Choir was a success. (Every year since, the group has made the choir camp a tradition, making a trek to Summer Music Camp in Black Mountain.) That led to Leonard Bernstein's *Mass* at Duke, and Duke gave the choir red robes that they still wear. In 1983 Graham got a call from the North Carolina Symphony to join in Benjamin Britten's *War Requiem*.

The group incorporated, and became the North Carolina Boys' Choir. In 1991 the choir added a chamber choir composed of former choir boys, singing tenor and bass. Graham also has a training choir to prepare boys for the concert choir, and they tour a different part of the country each year.

The choir performs at Duke University and usually does one Christmas performance each year. It is funded by parents, gifts, fundraisers, grants, and concert ticket sales. The headquarters of the North Carolina Boys' Choir is a block away from the University of North Carolina at Chapel Hill, in the Old St. Thomas More Catholic Church building.

Unlike most choirs, the North Carolina Boys' Choir rehearsals are open, so if ever you're in the area, stop in and give 'em a listen.

N★C FILM, MUSIC, AND DRAMA TRIVIA

Q. Lena Wilson, Vaudeville performer and jazz singer, was born in what North Carolina town?

A. Charlotte.

Q. What Winston-Salem actress had a starring role in *Kiss Me, Kate* and *Showboat*?

A. Kathryn Grayson.

Q. What Winston-Salem actress starred in *Beyond the Valley of the Dolls?*

A. Pam Grier.

Q. What producer and screenwriter, whose greatest films include *The Greatest Story Ever Told* and *The Cheyenne Social Club*, was born in 1929 in Charlotte?

A. James Lee Barrett.

Q. What was the last movie for Salisbury-born character actor Sidney Blackmer?

A. *Rosemary's Baby.*

Q. Where in Asheville was Peter Sellers's last movie, *Being There,* filmed?

A. The Biltmore House.

Q. What movie starring John Wayne was filmed in part in North Carolina?

A. *The Green Berets.*

Q. What Stephen King movie features more than a dozen eighteen-wheeler trucks running rampant through Wilmington?

A. *Maximum Overdrive.*

Q. What play was the first-ever outdoor drama in the United States?

A. Paul Green's play *The Lost Colony,* performed in North Carolina in 1937.

Q. What actor born in Roanoke Rapids is most famous for his roles in movies such as *From the Terrace, Advise and Consent,* and *Happy Birthday, Wanda June*?

A. George Grizzard.

Q. Who played the leading role in *Thunder Road,* filmed in North Carolina in 1958?

A. Robert Mitchum.

Q. What historic home in Southport was the setting for the movie *Firestarter*?

A. Orton Plantation.

Q. What famous director was born in Washington, North Carolina?

A. Cecil B. DeMille.

Q. What musical theater company based in Winston-Salem and composed of volunteers from the Triad area and students from the North Carolina School of Arts has been performing since 1978 and giving performances twice a year since 1984?

A. The Piedmont Opera Theatre.

12
Flora, Fauna, and
Natural Phenomena

Move Over, Rover—Guide Horses Are Here!

Janet and Donald Burleson in Kittrell have started the only school of its kind in the world: they train guide horses for sight-impaired people.

The Burlesons founded the nonprofit Guide Horse Foundation in 1999 as an alternative to guide dogs. Horses live longer than dogs, they point out, and thus have a longer service life.

"We were inspired by a little horse we had as a pet, Twinkie," Janet explains. "She made us start thinking how small horses like her could be used as service animals to help people." Janet says that pygmy horses, which usually grow to a height of two feet, are bred all over the country. The horses are donated to the foundation, and usually a dozen horses are training at a time. The Burlesons also have about twenty-five of their own horses, both miniature and Arabian.

How do they transport the horses? Janet explains that they flew Delta with a horse named Cuddles in March 2000—the first time a horse had ever flown in the passenger cabin of an airliner. "Delta was very cooperative, and let us come out to the airport and train the horse on the plane before the actual flight," says Janet.

The Burlesons say the pygmy horses are "amazingly simple" to train, and

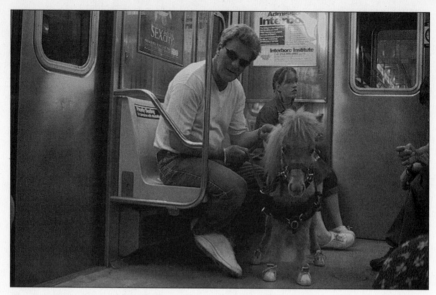

A guide horse assists a blind person on the New York City subway. (COURTESY JANET AND DONALD BURLESON, GUIDE HORSE FOUNDATION)

theirs have successfully learned more than twenty-three commands, including "load up," when boarding a taxi or automobile. Wearing a harness and leash, the tiny horses lead their masters in a manner similar to that of a guide dog. The Burlesons' first client was Dan Shaw of Ellsworth, Maine, and they now have a waiting list of people wanting their own version of Cuddles.

This Place Is the Cat's Meow

On fifty-five acres outside the town of Pittsboro, you will find an unusual place: the Carnivore Preservation Trust (CPT). It was established in 1981 by Michael Bleyman, Ph.D., a genetics professor at the University of North Carolina in Chapel Hill, who wanted a facility to breed endangered and threatened species that are vital to their ecosystems.

The animals he chose were primarily rodent killers, pollinators, or seed dispersers, whose roles are crucial to the environment. Species included caracals, servals, ocelots, and binturongs (also known as Asian bear cats, a little-known carnivore from southeast Asia). Dr. Bleyman also rescued many big cats, such as tigers and leopards, from horrible living conditions and provided them with a safe, comfortable home.

Dr. Bleyman died in 1997, and the current board of directors adopted a new mission: to provide sanctuary for endangered animals, primarily carnivores, and to promote education about their conservation. Today CPT houses around 160 threatened and endangered carnivores from ten different exotic species, including those mentioned above. The organization also finds homes for animals, placing them in other sanctuaries and zoos around the country. CPT is working on obtaining licensure from the U.S. Department of Agriculture and will seek accreditation with the Association of Sanctuaries.

CPT is funded by private donations and is a volunteer-based organization. Volunteers are encouraged to come and lend a hand.

Did You Know? In 1975 scientists in North Carolina reported the discovery of giant marine worms estimated to be more than 620 million years old—the oldest animal fossils in the United States.

The Wild Horses of Currituck Sound

Most towns have leash laws for pets—but in the coastal village of Corolla, the wild horses are pretty much free to roam. The horses are descended from what Southerners call "Old Family" and have been here longer than any human family in North Carolina.

Early in the 1500s, horse breeders on the Barbary Coast of northern Africa began to breed a special stock of horse that was above average in stamina. Impervious to heat and comfortable on sand, the animals also had an easy gait and an equally mild temperament. These horses became known as "Barb" horses, and Spanish explorers took them in their galleons as they explored the New World.

Eventually, because of shipwrecks or other reasons, some of these horses were left here. Because their genes had given them the amazing ability to withstand and even thrive under the extreme environmental conditions of the

Outer Banks, by the eighteenth century they were firmly established in Corolla.

Today, the horses are still relatively free, but with the coming of civilization, issues involving the free-roaming animals had to be addressed. The horses are now cared for through donations to the recently incorporated Corolla Wild Horse Fund, Inc., a nonprofit organization that works with the Currituck County officials, the North Carolina National Estuarine Research Reserve, the Currituck National Wildlife Refuge, and private landowners.

Former Horse Fund director Lloyd Childers is pleased with how the horses and people live together. The new plan, she says, keeps the horses out of the developed areas, lets them be periodically counted and evaluated, and ensures the protection of other plants and animals. She says that with significant grants from the William H. Donner Foundation of New York and under the new directors, Gene and Donna Snow, people and wild horses will continue to live in harmony.

The Corolla herd has been linked to Spanish origins, says Childers. "DNA studies confirmed their ancestry, and they have been recognized by the state of North Carolina as a significant historical and cultural resource. Now part of the scenery and culture of the Currituck Beach and Currituck Lighthouse includes glimpses of free-roaming horses, with their genetic roots in the Old World."

If ever you go see the wild horses of Currituck County, remember that you "herd" about them here first.

Did You Know? At the Fort Bragg Museum, you can see the stuffed remains of Barney, a small sun bear who became a mascot to troops serving in the Vietnam War.

In Spring a Tarheel's Fancy Turns to Turtles

Every year, beginning around the middle of May and lasting through August, a fascinating phenomenon occurs along the coast of North Carolina. By dark of night, huge female loggerhead sea turtles, each weighing three to five hundred pounds, lumber up the beaches where they were hatched. There they dig holes in the sand and lay their eggs—usually just over a hundred—and cover them with sand. After returning to the ocean, the mother loggerheads may return to their nesting spot to lay more eggs, usually at fourteen-day intervals for the entire nesting season.

As this occurs, hundreds of volunteers from North Carolina coastal communities walk the beaches. These volunteers, part of the Sea Turtle Conservation Project, protect the hatchling turtles as they emerge from their shells and struggle to get to the ocean.

Jean Beasley, who runs the Karen Beasley Sea Turtle Rescue and Rehabilitation Center in Topsail Island, explains that volunteers first look for the tracks of the mother turtle—which look like bulldozer tracks on the beach. Volunteers then rope the nests off so no one disturbs them. All nest sites, eggs, hatchlings, and sea turtles are protected under the Endangered and Threatened Species Act.

Dangers to baby turtles include raccoons, foxes, feral cats, and dogs. "The most common predatory danger for the hatchlings are ghost crabs," Beasley says. "They will wait outside the nest and attack the turtles as they emerge from their shells and struggle to cross the sand and get to the ocean." Once the turtles reach the ocean, they face sharks and predatory fish, as well as gulls and other birds that fly out over the water.

The job of the volunteer "turtle patrols" is limited to keeping predators away from the baby turtles as they struggle to get to the sea. "We have people come here, year after year, to help protect the hatchlings," Beasley says. "They plan their vacations around when the turtles hatch."

Now the project is international in scope, with sea turtle conservationists working all over the globe to protect this wide-ranging species.

Did You Know? The Great Dismal Swamp in northeastern North Carolina, which also reaches into Virginia, covers 750 square miles of North Carolina. It is an area of incredible biodiversity, created when the continental shelf made its last significant shift.

No Match for Mother Nature!

In 1915 developers in Hyde County had an ambition for Mattamuskeet Lake—they wanted to drain it and then farm and build upon the land. They didn't realize they were dealing with a very stubborn Mother Nature.

Developers forged ahead with the plan, a town called New Holland sprang up near the lake site, and the world's largest pumping station was built. The lake was drained, all right, and for a few years it was farmed successfully—but then heavy rains and nature had their say. The land again filled with water, and Lake Mattamuskeet returned.

At least the developers knew when they were beaten, and decided to make the best of things. With the help of the Civilian Conservation Corps, in 1934 the world's largest pumping station became Mattamuskeet Lodge, and in 1981 it was placed on the National Register of Historic Places. The lake itself, North Carolina's largest natural lake, was named Mattamuskeet National Wildlife Refuge.

The Amazing Great Smoky Mountains National Park

The Great Smoky Mountains National Park is one of the most unusual and beautiful places in the world. This 520,000-acre preserve ranges from wetlands to mountains, and is one of the most biologically diverse places on earth. More than 9,200 species of living things have been recorded there, but scientists say this represents only a small percentage; every year more species are recorded, adding to the already impressive list.

A naturalist counts beetles at the Great Smoky Mountains National Park. Over 9,200 species of flora and fauna have been recorded in the park so far. (PHOTO BY THE AUTHOR)

Here are just a few of the features that make the Great Smokies so great; some of these features are pointed out by guidebook author

Jeff Bradley [*The Tennessee Handbook: Including Nashville, Memphis, the Great Smoky Mountains, and Nutbush* (Chico, California: Moon Publications, 1999)].

★ Home to at least sixteen native mammals

★ The largest black bear preserve in the eastern United States

★ Habitat for about two hundred species of birds, including the scissor-tailed flycatcher, western kingbird, cliff swallow, tanager, and finch

★ The only habitat for Cain's reed-bent grass, Rugel's ragwort, and Jordan's red-cheeked salamander

★ Home to more than three hundred varieties of trees, more species than in all of Europe

★ Home to nine hundred varieties of wildflowers—more species than in any other place except Central China

About one-fourth of the acreage has never been disturbed; 95 percent of the park is forested, and there are more than seven hundred miles of streams. The park also preserves a unique collection of log buildings and maintains seventy-five historic structures depicting various aspects of pioneer life. It's an amazing place to visit!

The Cradle of Forestry

As a young boy growing up in Connecticut, Gifford Pinchot was encouraged by his father to become a forester, although it was not a profession in America at that time. Pinchot went on to study forestry in France (the United States had no forestry school), and in 1892 he came to the mountains of North Carolina to work on George Vanderbilt's Biltmore Forest Estate.

Next he became involved with the National Forest Commission, and in 1898 he was named chief of the Division of Forestry (later to become the Bureau of Forestry and, still later, the Forest Service). At the time, the

Department of the Interior controlled Forest Reserve lands. Pinchot and others worked diligently to have the Forest Reserves moved to the Department of Agriculture; this occurred in 1905, when the Forest Service was created. Pinchot became chief of this new Forest Service.

Under Pinchot, national forests grew from 56 million acres to 172 million acres by 1910, and forestry was elevated to a profession. Sharing his philosophy of the "greatest good for the greatest number," he taught his foresters to look at the long-term effects of their decisions. Pinchot also founded the Society of American Foresters, which first convened at his residence in Washington, D.C., in November 1900.

Today Pinchot is regarded as the father of American conservation because of his great and unrelenting concern for the protection of American forests and the environment. He popularized the concept of conservation of our natural resources.

What is amazing is the tremendous difference Pinchot made at a time when timberlands were thought to be virtually endless. At that time, anyone who took up the cause of the forest was thought a few branches shy of a tree. The concept of protecting a forest was a new one—people thought natural resources were meant to be used, and could never be used *up*.

The Class of 1905 at the Biltmore Forest School, the nation's first school of forestry, poses for a picture. (COURTESY FOREST HISTORY SOCIETY, DURHAM)

Pinchot's successor, Carl Alwin Schenck, began America's first school of forestry in 1898, then called the Biltmore Forest School. The campus has since been reconstructed and the land deeded to become part of the Pisgah National Forest. The original buildings are now part of a museum and educational center called the Cradle of Forestry in America.

Did You Know? The Forest History Society, a nonprofit research and educational organization established in 1946, is an international organization based in Durham. This society is the international leader in forest and conservation history and the primary contact for inquiries from around the world. Its library and archives contain the most comprehensive collection about forest and conservation history anywhere. Researchers, scientists, students, teachers, and journalists from around the globe use this information for their work. It is a truly unique resource.

The Kudzu Culture and Alternative Medicine

One "naturalized" North Carolina plant arrived in the United States as a vine used to shade the Japanese pavilion during the 1876 Centennial Exposition in Philadelphia. Americans hailed the kudzu as a "miracle" plant that would help prevent erosion and provide affordable feed for livestock. During the 1930s and 1940s, it was embraced as a farmers' and conservationists' panacea and planted throughout the Southern states, where it took a liking to the atmosphere.

Now North Carolina and neighboring states are draped with kudzu. It covers old barns, obliterates the words on roadside fences, and adorns interstate signs and anything moving too slowly to avoid its tendrils. It grows a foot a day in good conditions, so you can't just cut it back and think you're done. A hard frost stops it for a spell, but it never really goes away.

North Carolinians have just about given up fighting it, and have embraced it as part of their culture. Realizing that herbicides and mowing are either too expensive or just don't work, the people of the Tarheel State have found uses for the plant. Take seventy-three-year-old Edith Edwards, the self-proclaimed Kudzu Queen. She eats kudzu, adding it to such everyday dishes as casseroles, and attributes her longevity to this. She also makes hats and even Christmas trees out of the vines.

Kudzu has also found a use in alternative medicine—some medical researchers have found it can help fight alcoholism. Maybe it'll become another of North Carolina's cash crops. "Alternative medicine," of course, isn't new at all to Tarheels. In the old days, when you needed medicine, you just went out into the yard or the nearby woods to find the plant that would provide the cure.

Did You Know? The world's largest living Christmas tree is in Wilmington. The tree, a giant gnarled live oak that is 400 to 450 years old, stands on a bluff overlooking the Cape Fear River. Historical records state the tree once attained a height of 75 to 95 feet. "Hurricanes and ice storms have taken their toll on the tree, and reduced it somewhat in height," explained Parks and Recreation employee Tara Duckworth. "The tree is now about 50 feet tall and has a limb spread of 110 feet." It's given the traditional Christmas tree shape with help from a utility pole the city drove into the ground beside it. Every year, Wilmington Parks and Recreation staff decorate the tree using about seven thousand lights and two miles of twelve-gauge, industrial-strength wiring.

The world's largest living Christmas tree is in Wilmington. (COURTESY N.C. DIVISION OF TOURISM, FILM, AND SPORTS DEVELOPMENT)

Straight from a Sci-fi Flick

The small, greenish plant is about half a foot tall, with small white flowers and leaves ending in a blade-like form divided into two halves. The deceptively delicious-looking plant exudes a sweet-smelling fluid.

This can attract a fly, which in turn can attract a small frog, which soon becomes a meal for the plant. When the frog touches the outer portion of the leaves, the two halves snap shut, triggered by sensorial hairs. Long, sharp spines along the leaves' margins keep the frog from escaping. Inside the plant, sensors detect nitrogen in the frog's body, and digestive juices begin to dissolve the frog. Once digestion is complete, the innocent-looking leaves open again.

This plant is *Dionaea muscipula,* or Venus flytrap. Common to the Carolinas, the plant is often found around Carolina Beach State Park and other boggy places within a two-hundred-mile radius of Wilmington.

North Carolinians are proud of the plant that makes this state its home. Fascination abounds for the plant, and with good reason. It's one of a kind. "The Venus flytrap is the only plant I know that has two lobes that close over prey," said Jaime Amoroso, botanist with the North Carolina Natural

The Venus flytrap, a carnivorous plant, can be found around Carolina Beach State Park and in other boggy places. (COURTESY N.C. STATE MUSEUM OF NATURAL SCIENCES)

Heritage Program. "There are places where you can't walk without stepping on them, but the overall range has been shrinking due to habitat loss."

When you see the Venus flytrap in the wild, remember that it's a protected plant, so don't disturb it.

That Touch of Mink

Some people brake for yard sales. Some brake for flea markets. Others brake for bars. But naturalist Eric Stein brakes for roadkill. An interest in living animals led him to want to learn more about even dead creatures, and Stein's interest began to reveal something significant, at least to him. "I began to notice," he says, "that there were an awful lot of minks that were killed, more than many other types of roadkill."

Stein's further investigation revealed that minks are extremely common to Mecklenburg County. Those small, nocturnal, wily creatures, he says, are found not only in both North and South Carolina but are common across the United States.

Stein works for the Nature Museum in Charlotte, and in June 2001 to honor the numerous minks in North Carolina, the museum added a single male mink to its collection of animal exhibits. He answers to Murphy, and is a likable fellow.

Did You Know? Not until 1927 were hunting and fishing regulations under the authority of the State Gaming Commission, formed that year by the North Carolina General Assembly. Before then, the group responsible for establishing and administering those regulations was the Audubon Society!

Every Dog Has His (Work) Day

Patti Moran, president of Pet Sitters International based in King, had to "paws" one day when an idea came upon her. She knew about Take Your Daughters to Work Day. What about a Take Your Dog to Work Day?

The more Moran thought about it, the more she realized she wasn't barking up the wrong tree. In June 1999 the first such day was held. It has grown in popularity and now more than five thousand participants (and their pooches) from both the United States and Canada have at least *one* good day at the office each year. The goal, Moran says, is to call attention to the benefits dogs offer as pets, and "encourage adoptions from animal shelters, humane societies, and rescue clubs." The project enjoys the sponsorship of Iams Dog Food and Loews Hotel, among others.

Moran says everyone has a tail-wagging good time.

Mildred, the Mother Bear of Grandfather Mountain

Less than a hundred miles northeast of Asheville is the town of Linville, home to the only private park in the world designated by the United Nations as an International Biosphere Reserve. It's known as Grandfather Mountain because it resembles an old man's profile.

To be designated as an International Biosphere Reserve, an area must be home to a certain number of endangered plants and wildlife. (The exclusive list includes the Niagara Escarpment in Canada and the African Serengeti.) Grandfather Mountain and its environs support forty-two rare and endangered species, including about a dozen that are globally endangered. At last count there were 149 species of birds in the park. The United Nations periodically sends scientists to do studies of the endangered plants and wildlife, to learn how to preserve them for posterity.

Another amazing thing about Grandfather Mountain is one of the most colorful characters ever to come out of the woods—Mildred the Bear.

Mildred was brought from the Atlanta Zoo to Grandfather Mountain in 1968, and set free there by the Wildlife Commission to procreate, as the number of black bears in the area was diminishing rapidly. Mildred immediately set to work trying to charm the people of Linville—after all, she had been a "pet" of the Atlanta Zoo secretaries, and was not your typical wild black bear.

Over the years, Mildred had ten cubs of her own, and people were amazed at how gentle she was—she not only allowed humans near her cubs (generally a very dangerous undertaking), but also appeared to enjoy the many photos tourists took of her and her offspring. Then something happened that astonished the lay and scientific community alike.

Someone brought Mildred an abandoned cub named Hobo, hoping she might raise it, even though wild bears usually reject motherless cubs. Mildred, affectionate bear that she was, took the cub as one of her own. Next she adopted another abandoned cub named Punkin, then two siblings, Elizabeth and Walter.

Mildred became so popular that she is probably the most photographed bear in the world. She appeared in magazines such as *National Geographic, Outdoor Life,* and *Northwoods,* and in publications by the U.S. Forest Service.

Mildred lived longer than most bears in the wild, and died in her sleep as she dozed on January 1, 1993. She was just a few weeks shy of her twenty-seventh birthday, and was buried near an orchard on the mountain.

Mildred lives on in her descendants, the black bears of Grandfather Mountain, and in the museum. Thanks to talented sculptor Johnpaul Harris, you can see a bronze statue of Mildred and two of her cubs standing in the lobby of the Grandfather Mountain Nature Museum. Her three-acre former home, called Mildred the Bear Environmental Habitat, is accessible by foot.

Mildred the Bear lives on in her statue at the Grandfather Mountain Nature Museum—and in the many bears she has raised, who still reside in the forests nearby. (Reproduced with permission from Hugh Morton, photographer)

Whales, Birds, and Sharks, Oh My!

Five miles outside the coastal town of Aurora is a large phosphate mine. The area is rich in phosphate—a key ingredient in fertilizer—from the biodegradation of prehistoric marine life. Sometimes phosphate miners would come across intact fossils five million to fifteen million years old.

The town of Aurora has capitalized on these finds, displaying them in its Fossil Museum. Here you will find evidence that this part of North Carolina was once deep under the sea: on display are huge whale backbones, prehistoric bird bones, and gigantic shark teeth.

N★C FLORA AND FAUNA TRIVIA

Q. What is the name of the first cultivated wine grape, found in North Carolina?

A. The scuppernong.

Q. Who first recorded his findings of the scuppernong grape in his log book in 1524?

A. Florentine navigator Giovanni da Verrazano.

Q. When was the first commercial vineyard established in the state?

A. Medoc Vineyard was founded in Halifax County in 1835.

Q. How many commercial vineyards did North Carolina have in 2000?

A. More than two hundred and fifty.

Q. Which county is home to shallow, oval-shaped craters, called "Carolina Bays," said to have been created by a Pleistocene-era meteor shower?

Q. What zoo spearheaded a national crusade to help save the beleaguered animals in Afghanistan's Kabul Zoo?

A. The North Carolina Zoological Park (pictured above) in Asheboro.

(COURTESY N.C. DIVISION OF TOURISM, FILM, AND SPORTS DEVELOPMENT)

A. Bladen County.

Q. What world-class botanical garden of 450 acres was established in Belmont in 1991?

A. Daniel Stowe Botanical Garden.

Q. Approximately how many miles of rivers and streams lie within North Carolina's borders?

A. About forty thousand.

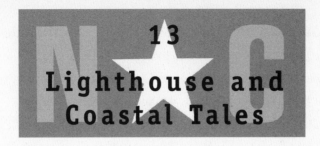

13
Lighthouse and Coastal Tales

The Mercurial Nature of the Outer Banks

Along North Carolina's coast, the Grim Reaper has been busy for hundreds of years, giving the treacherous waters its name, the "Graveyard of the Atlantic." The ocean has claimed several thousand oceangoing vessels since explorers and settlers first arrived on U.S. shores, and the North Carolina shoreline has always had a reputation for being extraordinarily dangerous, striking fear in even the most seasoned and intrepid crew.

Part of the reason for the extreme danger of these waters is the combination of current and wind. Prevailing North Atlantic winds are westerly but change direction quickly and with an exasperating lack of predictability. In the early days of sailing, ships traveling from Europe to America invited disaster if they sailed from January through March, when the winds were worse and even more unpredictable.

Then there's the hydrography (water flow and underwater landforms) to be considered. The hydrography of the area around Cape Hatteras called Diamond Shoals is mercurial. As a matter of fact, nautical topographers do not chart the hydrography of Diamond Shoals, due to the extremely changeable nature of the ocean floor.

The Ghost Ship of the "Graveyard of the Atlantic"

Hundreds of ships over the years have been lost to the area around Cape Hatteras and the treacherous waters of Diamond Shoals. One story in particular still haunts the seafaring history annals of North Carolina.

In the bitterly cold February winds of 1921, coast guardsmen saw in the dawning light a five-masted schooner under full sail. Run aground, her prow was deep in the sandy beach. The previous night's watchman at Cape Hatteras had told the incoming watchman it had been quiet, with no storm and nothing unusual. There was the ship, however, run firmly aground. No crew was visible, and no signs gave a clue about what could have caused it to run upon the shore with such force.

The ship was the *Carroll M. Deering*. Her lifeboats were gone, and a ladder swung from her side. No answering calls responded to distress whistles. When the seas calmed and low tide came in, the coast guards boarded the *Carroll M. Deering* and discovered that a cat was the only living thing aboard.

Equally disturbing was the fact that except for missing nautical papers, destroyed steering apparatus, and the rudder being left to swing freely, everything appeared as though the crew had just that moment stepped into their rooms or up on deck. The table was set with food, which had been partially eaten. The salon's lights still shone and the crew's bunks were all in order.

The ship had last been under the command of William B. Wormell, who had taken the vessel on a run to Rio de Janeiro, Brazil. Some rumors said that his crew had made mutinous plans and planned to do away with Wormell on the return voyage, while others said Wormell had been popular with his crew. Some speculated that pirates had taken the ship—but since it was returning with no goods aboard, what could they have possibly wanted?

By the time each story was investigated and each lead followed to a dead end, six departments of the U.S. government, from the navy to the Department of Commerce, had become involved. None had an answer about what had happened to the ship's crew.

Eventually, one of Cape Hatteras's inevitable storms came up, destroying what remained of the once-proud ship. No one knows what happened to her between South America and the cape, and the mystery of the *Carroll M. Deering* and her crew will forever remain just that—a mystery.

Did You Know? Until the 1920s the Outer Banks were relatively isolated, connected by ferries to the rest of North Carolina. Ferries were vital to life in the small communities of this area, and have helped tourists visit this area so rich in history. Although privately owned at first, in 1934 the state of North Carolina began subsidizing the ferry services, and in 1947 the Department of Transportation established the North Carolina Ferry Division. Now based in Morehead City, it administers the largest ferry system in the United States, taking residents, fishing enthusiasts, and visitors by the millions to unwind along the unspoiled beaches, fish the inlets and bays, and take in the ambience of the colorful area known as the Outer Banks.

The Surfmen and Fonzie the Lifesaving Dog

In 1873 Congress established the U.S. Lifesaving Service. Its purpose was to set up lifesaving stations along the coast, and to employ people to staff the stations, especially surfmen (men who patrolled the coast on foot or horseback, looking for ships in distress). Ultimately, seven such stations were built at approximately seven-mile intervals along the coast of the area known as Chicamacomico.

There is one such station still intact today. In the village of Rodanthe on Hatteras Island, you will find Chicamacomico Lifesaving Station, which was one of the first stations to be built on the coastline of the Tarheel State. The buildings on the site constitute the most complete surviving U.S. Lifesaving Service/Coast Guard station complex in the country, and the grounds have been made into a museum open to the public.

But there's more to the story than that. This is a family tale—the heart-warming kind with a dog in it.

For lots of folks on the coast, lifesaving, patrolling the shore, and taking care of beacons and lighthouses were a family tradition. Take Levene Midgett, who took over the Chicamacomico Lifesaving Station around 1911, shortly after the death of the previous keeper—his cousin, who was know as Captain Ban Midgett. The Midgett family held a sort of monopoly on lifesaving stations in the area. In fact, it was difficult around Chicamacomico *not* to hire someone whose last name was Midgett. In 1970 the U.S. Census showed that 103 of the 266 inhabitants of the three villages of Chicamacomico were Midgetts.

In the early 1940s Levene had a dog named Fonzie, a black Labrador retriever who was noted and loved for being a "surf-dog." When Levene hoisted the U.S. flag at the station every morning, Fonzie would stand up tall (locals say "as close to standing at attention as a dog could get") and then put his paws on the surfmen's line-throwing equipment, ready to go to work. Historian Robert Huggett says, "The dog always did as he was told; it got to be where the surfmen thought Fonzie was a surfman—and so did Fonzie. During World War II he was taken on patrols of the beaches, looking for beached mines and anything that might have come from a ship."

Fonzie died of old age around 1952. He's buried in the Midgett family cemetery, about 150 yards from the lifesaving station. Fonzie was given a military burial with full honors of the Coast Guard. (Huggett says, "He was probably the only dog on the island to be given a military funeral.") His grave, which you can still see today, is marked with a decommissioned mine.

Did You Know? The U.S. Coast Guard is responsible for about 167 manned lighthouses, 12,000 unmanned lights, 26,000 buoys and other nautical navigational aids.

Beacons of Light and Life

For sailors everywhere, but especially around the shoreline of the North Atlantic and North Carolina in particular, lighthouses are a beacon of hope and life, especially when extreme danger is imminent. Before the appearance of lighthouses, bonfires on shore illuminated the way for some of the first sailors.

For nearly two hundred years after North Carolina was settled, its shores had no lighthouses. Finally, after losing hundreds of ships and countless lives to the "Graveyard of the Atlantic," the U.S. government, still in its fledgling stages, passed legislation to build lighthouses in 1793.

The first was the Bald Head Lighthouse in 1795, followed by Ocracoke in 1795 and Cape Hatteras in 1802. After the Civil War, Congress established the Lighthouse Board, which oversaw construction of new lighthouses every forty miles along the coast. (The Lighthouse Board later became the Lighthouse Service and is now a part of the U.S. Coast Guard.)

For those whose feet never leave dry land, lighthouses continue to capture the imagination. Originally fueled by kerosene and now equipped with sophisticated technology, lenses, and radar equipment, six lighthouses now illuminate the shoreline along the Tarheel State, from Bald Head Island in the south to Currituck in the north.

If lighthouses could speak, what tales they would tell!

★ **Cape Hatteras Lighthouse** was built in 1870. It stands 193 feet tall, making it the highest in the United States. Long considered the guardian of the treacherous Diamond Shoals, the area around Cape Hatteras and its lighthouse is now a National Seashore. For some years, the lighthouse was threatened by the waters over which it stood guard. Waves pounded away at the foundation of this 4,800-ton giant of granite, brick, marble, iron, brass, and bronze. Finally the shoreline was only one hundred and twenty feet away from the base of the old lighthouse. One major hurricane and the old landmark could be doomed.

The National Park Service had been reinforcing the beachfront with sandbags, but in early 1999 it began preparing to follow the recommendation of the National Academy of Sciences that the tower be loaded up and rolled to a new site up the beach where the lighthouse could guard the cape in safety.

Workers first separated the lighthouse from its foundation using a heavy-duty diamond-wire saw. It was then raised on one hundred hydraulic jacks and steel beams slid underneath. Seven additional steel beams fitted with roller dollies supported lighthouse and frame. Five hydraulic rams nudged the lighthouse down a track, as the monolith made its way to its new home a half-mile up the beach.

Workers moved the lighthouse at a top speed of one foot per minute, with engineers using computers to constantly check the proper placement of the jacks to keep the structure level. Workers lubricated the travel tracks with bars of Ivory soap—which, like lard, is a time-honored nautical tool for instances such as this.

Finally the lighthouse arrived at its new location on July 9, 1999, two weeks ahead of schedule and without even so much as the hint of a crack in the mortar. Thanks to professional lighthouse movers of local and national renown, the most famous lighthouse in America had arrived at its new home.

★ **Currituck Beach Lighthouse,** sometimes referred to as Whalehead, is located at the village of Corolla, north of Kitty Hawk. Standing 158 feet tall, the lighthouse was built in 1875 to light the last remaining dark forty-mile stretch of the south Atlantic coastline between Cape Henry Lighthouse in Virginia and Bodie Island Lighthouse. There's a special reason for the popularity of this red-brick lighthouse: in and around the grounds you can see and hear the wild horses of Corolla, which enhance the romantic feeling of the area. More than eighty-three thousand people visit Currituck Beach Lighthouse annually.

The red-brick Currituck Beach Lighthouse is visited by more than eighty-three thousand people each year. (COURTESY N.C. DIVISION OF TOURISM, FILM, AND SPORTS DEVELOPMENT)

★ **Bald Head Lighthouse,** built in 1817, is the oldest lighthouse in North Carolina. "Old Baldy," as it is affectionately called, is an octagon-shaped structure on Bald Island, and has long been used to guide ships around the treacherous Cape Fear and Frying Pan Shoals. A previous version of the lighthouse, built in 1796, was torn down and replaced with the existing lighthouse. Deactivated in 1935, it still stands proudly at its original ninety feet and is now a museum. A rewarding panoramic view awaits those who brave the 112 wooden steps to the top of the lighthouse. You can gain access to Smith Island and Old Baldy Lighthouse by boat.

★ **Oak Island Lighthouse,** 169 feet tall, is on the lower southeastern coast and is the newest addition to the lighthouses lining the Maryland, Virginia, and North Carolina coastline. Built in the 1950s, it is also the brightest lighthouse in the United States and the second brightest in the world (the first is in Calais, France). Oak

Island replaced the previous Cape Fear Lighthouse in 1958; it is accessible by a bridge connecting the island to the nearby city of Southport. When Oak Island opened, the old caretaker of the Cape Fear Lighthouse, Charlie Swan, who had maintained that beacon for fifty-five years, threw the switch in a lighting ceremony.

★ **Price's Creek Lighthouse,** built around 1848 as one of a string of beacons along a twenty-five-mile stretch of the Cape Fear River, lies abandoned and unused about two miles from Southport. It lies on land now owned by Archer Daniel Midland (ADM), a chemical company making citric acid. Although you can't tour the lighthouse, plans are underway to turn the beacon over to the city of Southport, so tours may be possible in the future. In the meantime, you can see the twenty-foot-tall lighthouse tower from the ferry as it crosses the Cape Fear River between Southport and Fort Fisher. During the Civil War, this lighthouse was a signal station for the Confederates and the only means of communication across the Cape Fear River. Confederate soldiers rendered Price's Creek inoperable after the second battle of Fort Fisher in 1865.

★ **Ocracoke Lighthouse,** built in 1823, stands in the fishing village of Ocracoke Island, an area once frequented by the notorious pirate Blackbeard. It's one of the oldest continually operating lighthouses in the country. The adjacent lighthouse keeper's house was built to withstand inclement coastal weather, with sixteen-inch brick walls covered with whitewashed mortar. The seventy-six-foot lighthouse still is whitewashed, using a recipe recommended by the U.S. Lighthouse Board: Take unslaked lime, and add boiling water, salt, powdered Spanish whiting, and ground rice. Add more boiling water and clear glue. Mix until smooth and apply while hot.

★ **Bodie Island Lighthouse** represents the third attempt to place a lighthouse on Bodie Island (pronounced "body," one legend says because of so many bodies that washed up on shore), north of Hatteras Island at Oregon Inlet. The first lighthouse, standing at the rocky shore of the island, leaned so much that it was irreparably out of alignment. The second was blown up by Confederate soldiers (rather than let it fall into Union hands). The third and existing structure stands at 150 feet; construction began in 1871 and was completed in 1872. The lighthouse keeper's quarters have been converted into a visitors' center and museum under the management of Cape Hatteras National Seashore. The beautiful lighthouse with its distinctive black-and-white bands is popular with tourists, historians, and naturalists, and accessible by a bridge to the island.

★ **Cape Lookout Lighthouse,** built in 1859 on the Core Banks east of Beaufort, has helped sailors navigate the treacherous ten-mile stretch of waters known as Lookout Shoals. On the lands of the Core Banks in the nineteenth century, a small village called Diamond City thrived, with an economy based on the whaling industry. Fierce storms and raging tides drove the settlers to move west to nearby Shackleford Banks, but historians write of human skeletons found in the area, exposed by the constantly shifting sand. The 163-foot-tall lighthouse can be reached by boat from Harkers Island, Beaufort, or Morehead City.

Perfect Storm, Perfect Heroes

On October 25, 1991, the ninety-five-foot schooner *Anne Kristine* set sail from New York for Bermuda. The 123-year-old ship was the oldest continuously used sailing vessel in the world, launched from Norway in 1868. None of the crew had a premonition that their lives would be in grave danger in less than thirty-six hours.

The day after their departure, the crew of seven men and two women, including the ship's new owners, Norman and Mary Ann Baker, was alerted to the storm brewing about five hundred miles southeast. Captain Joey Gelband turned the ship's bow west to try and sail around the storm (which was to become Hurricane Grace). But a second storm was coming toward the *Anne Kristine*: the nor'easter that Sebastian Junger wrote about in *The Perfect Storm*, which was later made into a movie. The two storm systems were heading toward each other, with no escape for the ship and her crew. By October 29 the storm had peaked, and the crew was in a desperate situation.

The crew had changed course to head inland, but ever-increasing waves

Did You Know? Lighthouses are often painted with different designs and colors and even built in varying shapes to increase their visibility and to help sailors determine their own location as they sail along the coast. The most favored colors are highly contrasting black and white, sometimes in a band, diamonds, or even a spiral candy-cane design. Each lighthouse also has a different type of beacon, with each assigned its own character of light, called a code. Each lighthouse's beacon has variations in intensity, color, beacon elevation, and frequency of the flash.

Bodie Island, Cape Lookout, and Hatteras Lighthouses (left to right) are painted in different patterns of black and white to help sailors identify them. (COURTESY N.C. DIVISION OF TOURISM, FILM, AND SPORTS DEVELOPMENT)

pounded the *Anne Kristine* and washed over her decks, and her pumps could not keep up. As she began taking on water, the captain called his first "Mayday." Elizabeth City's Coast Guard Station sent out a C-130 (a military air transport aircraft) with dewatering pumps, followed by two new Jayhawk helicopters. The pumps would be dropped so the crew could use them to try to keep the vessel from sinking, and then the helicopters would pick up the crew.

This was no ordinary rescue, even for such a seasoned helicopter pilot as Lieutenant Commander Paul Lange. He ran low on fuel and was forced to refuel on the heaving decks of the USS *America*, in thirty-foot seas and fifty-mile-per-hour winds, off the coast of Cape Henry, Virginia, a feat in itself.

Arriving at the crippled and pounded *Anne Kristine*, Lange discovered that the pumps carried by the C-130 had all missed their mark, and the second rescue helicopter had not arrived. It was up to him and his crew to rescue the nine people, in fifty-foot seas and winds gusting at eighty miles an hour.

Dropping down to lower his rescue basket, Lange had to be ready to gain altitude rapidly to escape the rushing waves. Often the waves missed the bottom of the helicopter by inches, and the spray from one rogue wave washed into the open doorway.

Incredibly, Lange and his crew managed to rescue all nine crew members. As they pulled Helband into the helicopter, the *Anne Kristine* foundered, rolled on her side, and slipped under the waves. As Lange and his loaded helicopter returned home, he met the missing helicopter and they flew back to base together.

Lange and his crew, David Morgan, Duane Jones, and John A. Julian, received several awards for their bravery, including the 1991 Helicopter Heroism Award. Lange also received the Distinguished Flying Cross.

In one of the most monstrous storms ever to hit the eastern seaboard, Lange and his crew had flown nearly three hundred miles offshore to effect a rescue. Their work that night, in the "storm of the century," exemplifies what it is to be a hero.

N★C LIGHTHOUSE AND COASTAL TRIVIA

Q. Who was the first commissioner of the U.S. Bureau of Lighthouses?

A. George R. Putnam.

Q. When was the Lighthouse Bureau abolished, and by what presidential act?

A. In 1939 the Presidential Reorganizational Act abolished the Lighthouse Bureau and made the U.S. Coast Guard the lighthouse authorities.

Q. What is the oldest lifesaving station in North Carolina?

A. The Coast Guard Station in Oregon Inlet.

Q. What county and military base were dubbed the first "storm-ready community" by the National Weather Service in 2000?

A. Onslow County and Camp Lejeune, the Marine Corps base located there.

Q. Who was the force behind the creation of the Marine Revenue Cutter Service, the precursor to the Coast Guard, on August 4, 1790?

A. Alexander Hamilton.

Q. What retirement home was created for sailors in the town of Sealevel?

A. Snug Harbor. Although the home also open its doors to "landlubbers," it is still predominantly made up of "old salts," both male and female.

14
Speech, Food, and Fascinating Cultural Tidbits

The Way Things Are Said

From the mountains of west North Carolina to the Piedmont or heartland to the coast, the speech patterns of the residents are downright fascinating.

The coastal residents have accents reflecting their roots as well as their geography. On Harker's Island, for instance, people have retained speech patterns and accents reminiscent of the jolly old England of the Elizabethan era, especially noticeable when they say things such as "high tide" (which they pronounce *hoigh toyed*).

In the mountains, people have descended from folks who were educated in Shakespearean English—you may hear this referred to as Appalachian English or mountain English. Speech patterns in these relatively isolated pockets come from the early settlers from the British Isles in the late seventeenth and early eighteenth centuries, and people retained their linguistic roots because of the isolation, despite the passage of time. You can still hear these speech patterns today, double negatives and all—but rather than reflecting a lack of education, these speech patterns reflect a long history.

Mountain English uses *hit* for "it" and *we-uns* as another form of "us." The word "done" occurs often, as in "They done got married," or "That pig's done gone and got tangled up in the barbed wire." Other examples are using *a* as a prefix, as in "I was a-fixing to go to the store," or saying "I knowed it" instead of "I knew it." Just keep in mind that this usage is not evidence of ignorance, or you might find yourself a-fixing to get in a fight.

In the Piedmont area, due to an influx of people with varied ethnic and linguistic backgrounds, you will hear a little bit of everything. The further south you go, the more likely you will be to hear speech with a drawl, and the severity of the drawl does not seem to depend on how other members of the family speak.

Family is important to Tarheel natives. The further back you can trace your family roots, the better. A native might say proudly that he is "fourteenth-generation Tidewater aristocracy," and that sort of attention to familial roots is part of the Tarheel tradition and culture.

Wherever you ramble in the Tarheel State, be assured that in very few places on this planet will you find warmer, friendlier, more accommodating folks—who are also such wonderful cooks! That combination has been cause for many non-natives to set up permanent housekeeping in the Tarheel State.

The Vilest-Smelling, Sweetest-Tasting Weed

Every first Sunday in May, the American Legion of Haywood County has its annual Ramp Festival. The ramp is a wild plant of the allium family (similar to an onion), which grows only in the Appalachian Mountains. In the spring the mountain people dig up the ramps, clean them, and cook them in all sorts of dishes.

For North Carolinians, the fact that the ramp grows only in this limited area makes it special enough to celebrate, with craft shows, lots of live bluegrass and country music, and of course plenty of ramps to eat (and they're in just about everything except maybe the ice cream).

American Legion member Mark Leopard says that ramps taste "real good" in meatloaf. Here's Mark's recipe, in his words:

Mark Leopard's Meatloaf with Ramps

You take the ramps, wash 'em real good, dice 'em up, and use 'em instead of the onions called for in your meatloaf recipe. You can even use the ramp tops. Mix 'em up with your other meatloaf ingredients and bake it as you usually would. They add a little bit of an onion-garlic taste to it.

Can't Win? Try This Contest!

Ayden has an Annual Collard Festival every September. This includes the crowning of the Collard Queen and a Collard Green Eating Contest. This one-day event is open to anyone with an appetite.

The contest rules are simple: the person who eats the most collard greens in thirty minutes (without throwing up) wins. The winning record, set a few years ago, is seven and three-quarters pounds.

One-of-a-kind Festivals

The Tarheel State boasts many unusual festivals and contests—too many to mention them all. But here's a sampling to whet your curiosity:

★ Lizard Lick started an annual event featuring lizard races to gain some recognition.

★ Spring Hope wasn't content with simply having a Pumpkin Festival; it has an annual National Pumpkin Festival (guess it's the gardener's version of the World Series).

★ Newport has its annual Pig Cooking Contest, said to be the largest such cooking contest anywhere in the world.

★ Banner Elk doesn't have an "elk" contest, but every October it does have a Woolly Worm Festival.

★ Saluda has a Coon Dog Day (which includes a barking contest, dogs only, please) every July.

★ Spivey's Corner has a National Hollerin' Contest, which attracted so much attention that contestants have appeared on *The Tonight Show*.

★ Oriental, on the coast, has an annual Croaker Queen contest. (A croaker is a fish—and they really do croak!)

★ Clinton hosts the Eastern North Carolina Ugly Pickup Truck Contest.

★ Beech Mountain has its annual Garbage Day to celebrate the purchase of the town's first garbage truck (in 1982).

Did You Know? Formed in 1861, Transylvania County was *not* named after the Romanian town of Bram Stoker's writings, but from the Latin words *trans* and *sylva,* which mean "across a wood." But when an advertising agency suggested that the county would draw more tourists if it changed its name to something with less frightening connotations, the Transylvanians "saw red." Their response culminated in a festival celebrating the unique name. Since 1987 every Halloween (or the nearest Saturday), Transylvanians have held their own Halloweenfest, with a costume contest, parade, trick-or-treating at the downtown merchants, and a Flight of the Vampire five-kilometer race in which some runners dress as vampires. Many out-of-towners show up for the festival. So much for the advertising agency's suggestion!

A Seasonal Delicacy of the Finned Variety

Every year, from January through April, river herring surge from the Atlantic Ocean and up the Roanoke, Chowan, Tar-Pamlico, and other rivers in eastern North Carolina to spawn in those quiet and relatively protected waters. This seasonal occurrence sees a burst of human activity, as thousands of folks catch herring and cook them in makeshift "cook-up shacks" thrown up alongside riverbanks. The Cypress Grill, located in the tiny, two-red-light town of Jamesville, has cooked and served up herring to generations of diners.

The building itself is nondescript, a shack of weathered board-and-batten cypress siding, with shuttered windows and a tin roof. The Cypress Grill, which is open only as long as the herring are running, is reputed to be the only seasonal herring shack in the Roanoke region.

You can count on your herring being fresh at the Grill: at "dawn-thirty" every morning, Leslie Gardner launches his skiff to net the foot-long delicacy. Leslie, along with his wife, Sally, and long-time cook Julia Price, fries up around five hundred herring every day.

"You can have your herring fried a number of ways," says Sally. "'Sunny-side-up' is barely fried. If you like your fish cooked until it's a deep golden brown, you would ask for it to be 'cremated.'"

The herring are a part of the culture around here and serve as a seasonal reminder to old-timers who in poorer times lived off fish and collard greens. Now you can taste what life was like back then—only now, the herring are served up with freshly brewed iced tea and lots of homemade pie for dessert.

You'll be welcome at the Cypress Grill—just make sure you visit during herring season.

Corn, One of the Four Food Groups

Corn is one of the most abundant crops grown for human consumption in the Tarheel State, and everyone, it seems, has a specific way to cook it. Diane and John Fitzgerald are transplants from New York, living just outside Canton. John went to a fancy chef's school up north, and when he came to his senses and moved to North Carolina, he brought with him the perfect way to boil corn. Here is his tried-and-true, always-delicious recipe:

John Fitzgerald's Boiled Corn

Pick the corn yourself just before you plan to shuck it, or buy it from a farmer so you know it's freshly picked. Start a big pan of water boiling, enough to cover the ears, then shuck the corn. When the water is at a rolling boil, put the ears in. Bring it to a boil again, then cover it and turn it off.

It can sit like this in the water, and it's important that you don't drain it until you're ready to eat it. It doesn't overcook, it stays juicy and fresh-tasting. You can even leave it in the water overnight and have some cold boiled corn for breakfast. It hardly needs butter at all.

An Eagle's Nest—for Humans

In lovely New Bern, just a stone's throw from the Tryon Palace, is an old bed and breakfast known as the Aerie. An aerie is an eagle's nest, and this is about the most comfortable and inviting "nest" in North Carolina. Besides running a top-notch establishment, Donna and Doug Bennett are excellent cooks. Donna is also a certified herbalist and her gardens bear this out (because of the great climate and fertile soil, herbs grow like proverbial weeds). Here's a recipe using some traditional North Carolina herbs she grows.

Italian Herbed Eggs

2 to 3 eggs
Fresh oregano, chopped
Fresh basil, chopped
Parmesan or Romano cheese, grated
Fresh chives, chopped

Mix equal amounts of basil and oregano in a small bowl. Put a pinch of the blended herbs in a bowl. Add eggs and scramble. Sprinkle in cheese to taste, and cook the eggs in a frying pan as usual. Garnish with the chives. Serve hot. Makes 1 serving—increase amounts for more servings.

The Seafood Capital of the World

Residents of the town of Calabash and the surrounding area have been cooking seafood since the introduction of the fishhook and net. They have a long-standing tradition of outdoor oyster roasts, which moved indoors as the years passed. They pride themselves on a secret style of frying seafood, referred to as "Calabash-style cooking."

One Chamber of Commerce staff member tried to describe what sets this place's style of seafood cooking apart. "The taste of Calabash cooking isn't so much about the flavor or spices," she says. "It's the way the seafood is prepared. It's lightly battered and quickly fried, which gives it a special taste that's not heavy." Calabash, known as "the Seafood Capital of the World," has a population of around two hundred and is known for its extraordinary number of restaurants—at least one for every ten people. You won't go hungry here, that's for sure.

Brunswick County resident Geneva Crawford has put together a cookbook called *Savory Treasures from the Sea and Beyond* (Ocean Isle Beach, N.C.: Savory Treasures, Out My Kitchen Window, Inc., 1999) with more than 150 recipes from families old and new to the area. Here are two that she thought reflected the taste of Calabash in particular and coastal North Carolina in general.

Slick Vic's Carolina Crab Cakes

(Contributed by Vic Gillespie, Holden Beach)

> 1 pound lump crabmeat
>
> 2 tablespoons mayonnaise
>
> 1 small onion, finely chopped
>
> 10 saltines, crushed
>
> 1 teaspoon mustard
>
> 1 to 2 dashes Texas Pete Hot Sauce
>
> 1 egg
>
> ½ stick butter

Mix all the ingredients except the butter, and form into 8 crab cakes. Melt half the butter in a heavy frying pan. Fry 4 crab cakes until golden brown. Repeat with the remaining crab cakes. Serve the crab cakes with coleslaw and fried potatoes, and perhaps a glass of white wine. Makes 8 crab cakes.

Shrimp Curry

(Contributed by Gigi Hutcherson, Calabash)

3 tablespoons oil

1 large onion, finely chopped

1 teaspoon fresh garlic, finely chopped

1 teaspoon chopped fresh gingerroot

¼ teaspoon ground black pepper

1 teaspoon curry powder

½ teaspoon cumin

1 teaspoon cayenne

1 large tomato, peeled and diced

1 teaspoon salt

2 tablespoons vinegar

1 pound shrimp, peeled and deveined

Heat the oil in a saucepan. Sauté the onion, garlic, and ginger until soft and brown. Add the pepper, curry powder, cumin, and cayenne, and cook for 4 minutes. Add the tomato, salt, and vinegar. Cover and simmer until the tomato is reduced to pulp. Add the shrimp and stir well. Cover and simmer until the shrimp are done, about 5 to 10 minutes. Serve with white rice. Makes approximately 6 servings.

Roasted Oysters, Tarheel Style

Marilyn Coleman Howarth, a granddaughter of Lucy Coleman, is one of a long line of seafood cooks. She says that when growing up, she and other children earned tips by shucking oysters for the customers at her grandmother's restaurant. "We would shuck the oysters right at the table using a wooden-handled knife, using the knife to pull the oysters out and put them in a bowl for the customers," she says. Sometimes they had oyster-shucking contests.

Here is how she describes the classic way to roast oysters:

Lucy Coleman's Classic Roast Oysters

First wash the oysters to make sure there's no sand or mud on them, then line the bottom of a flat pan with them. Cover the pan with a little water, maybe half a cup just enough to keep the oysters from burning. Cover it with either a lid or a dishcloth to keep the steam on the inside. Steam them on medium heat; they open as they get done. If they cook too much, they'll dry. Some people like 'em juicy and some like their oysters drier. You serve the oysters with cocktail sauce, drawn butter, and hot sauce. Some people mix their own combinations using horseradish, ketchup and hot sauce—whatever your taste buds tell you. You always have a cold drink like iced tea or cola with it. And saltine crackers, too.

N★C Strange . . . but true

The Real Mrs. Calabash

Every time he closed one of his television or radio shows, the late Jimmy Durante would say, "Good night, Mrs. Calabash, wherever you are."

There apparently was no real Mrs. Calabash, but Lucy Coleman ran a restaurant in Calabash where Durante and his entourage stopped in for a bite in 1940. When Durante left, he reportedly turned to Coleman and said, "Good night, Mrs. Calabash," the phrase that became part of his shows from then on.

The good news is that the restaurant still exists. Although Lucy passed away in 1989, her son Virgil still runs Coleman's Original Calabash.

Lucy Coleman's cooking inspired Jimmy Durante's closing phrase and put Calabash on the map.
(CONTRIBUTED BY MARILYN HOWARTH)

Did You Know? North Carolina raises more turkeys and more sweet potatoes than any other state. Two cities hold festivals to celebrate this: Raeford has a Turkey Festival, and Smithfield a Ham and Yam Festival.

The Center of the (Barbecue) Universe

In Lexington in the 1920s, four men—Jesse Swicegood, Sid Weaver, Will Johnson, and Warner Stamey—noticed that when the courthouse was in session, the crowds were enough to support an eating establishment or two. They thought immediately of barbecue, and every day court was in session, the four set up their tents and cooked barbecue over makeshift cinder block pits.

Barbecue is served with red slaw and hush puppies at the Lexington Barbecue Festival.
(COURTESY N.C. DIVISION OF TOURISM, FILM, AND SPORTS DEVELOPMENT/LTA)

The particular style of barbecuing eventually became famous and is known as Lexington-style barbecue. This is different than in eastern North Carolina where the pig is cooked whole and served with white or yellow slaw. In the Piedmont area of Lexington, chefs cook shoulders and serve the barbecue with red slaw and hush puppies. Many of these chefs eschew electricity and gas, and cook the pork over hickory coals.

Those tents are gone, but Lexington has become known around the world for its barbecue and has more barbecue houses per capita than anyplace else (at last count, sixteen for a population of about sixteen thousand). And, yes, they still cook with hickory coals.

Lexington celebrates its barbecue-cooking heritage every third week in October, serving barbecue on the town square and entertaining people with pig races.

Here's a slaw recipe from Wayne "Honey" Monk, owner of one of the oldest such family-owned barbecue restaurants in Lexington.

Wayne "Honey" Monk's Famous Slaw

10 pounds sugar
8 ounces salt
8 ounces black pepper
¼ teaspoon cayenne
100 pounds medium-chopped cabbage
6 quarts ketchup
½ gallon vinegar

Mix the sugar, salt, black pepper, and cayenne into the chopped cabbage. Let sit for 20 minutes. Add the ketchup and vinegar and mix well. Refrigerate as long as possible before serving. (*Note:* This recipe is intended for a very large, restaurant-sized crowd. You may want to cut it down a bit when making this slaw for your own dinner table!)

North Carolina's First, Biggest, and Most

Here are some North Carolina features that give Tarheels bragging rights:

★ **World's only gourd museum:** the Marvin and Mary Johnson Gourd Museum in Fuquay-Varina, in Wake County.

★ **Highest swinging footbridge in the United States:** on Grandfather Mountain in Linville, more than a mile above sea level.

★ **Largest unsupported dome in North America:** the elliptical dome of the Basilica of St. Lawrence Church in Asheville. Made entirely of tiles, it measures eighty-two by fifty-eight feet and is a beautiful, awe-inspiring sight.

★ **Rockfish Capital of the World:** the city of Weldon, where the rockfish spawn upriver every spring in the Roanoke River, and anglers from all over come to try their luck.

★ **Largest open-face granite quarry in the world:** outside Mount Airy in Surry County; it measures one mile long and 1,800 feet wide.

The world's only fossil of an Acrocanthosaurus (right) makes its home at the North Carolina Museum of Natural Science. (COURTESY N.C. MUSEUM OF NATURAL SCIENCES)

★ **World's largest painting:** a cyclorama of the Battle of Gettysburg, in Winston-Salem. (The 22 x 376-foot painting is in need of restoration and is in storage at Wake Forest University.)

★ **World's only Acrocanthosaurus fossil:** in the North Carolina Museum of Natural Sciences, Raleigh. (This you've got to see!)

★ **Only Southeast museum devoted to the study of world cultures:** the Museum of Anthropology at Wake Forest University.

★ **Highest waterfall in the eastern United States:** Whitewater Falls in Sapphire. Although it's much narrower than Niagara, it beats it in height by 200 feet, with a total drop of 411 feet.

★ **Largest ammunitions depot in the United States:** Point Military Ocean Depot, near Southport.

★ **Oldest active military reservation:** Fort Johnston, in Southport, dating back to 1750.

★ **World's largest Ten Commandments:** in Murphy, erected by the Church of God of Prophecy, and measuring three hundred feet wide.

★ **Christmas tree capital of the world:** Avery County, which produces more Christmas trees of every kind than anywhere else.

★ **First national military park at a Revolutionary War site:** the Guilford County Courthouse National Military Park in Greensboro.

★ **First planetarium at a university:** Morehead Planetarium (part of the University of North Carolina at Chapel Hill).

★ **Only rural doctor museum in America:** the Country Doctor Museum in Bailey, dedicated to the life of the rural medical practitioner in the 1800s.

★ **Largest unincorporated U.S. city:** Kannapolis, population thirty-five thousand.

★ **Largest U.S. university-related research park:** Research Triangle Park in Durham, also home to many companies engaged in advanced scientific research and development.

★ **Second-oldest river in the world:** the New River, which flows in North Carolina and West Virginia, and is about one billion years old (only the Nile is older). Mapmakers didn't discover it until they had already completed their cartography of the region.

★ **World's largest frying pan:** in Rose Hill. The pan measures fifteen feet in diameter and is used during the town's Fall Jamboree Festival, and reportedly can hold more than 250 chickens at one time.

N★C CULTURAL TRIVIA

Q. Where was North Carolina's first newspaper established?

A. New Bern.

Q. What North Carolina community with a huge holiday lighting display has become known as Christmas Town?

A. McAdenville.

Q. What town is called the Smithsonian of the South and why?

A. Raleigh, because of its many free and family-friendly things to do.

Q. Where is the first public boarding school for mathematically and scientifically gifted high school students?

A. Durham, known as the North Carolina School of Science and Mathematics.

Q. New York drops a ball on New Year's Eve. What similar event happens in Raleigh? (Hint: it is known as the City of Oaks.)

A. At midnight a huge copper acorn is dropped in the middle of Moore Square, downtown.

Q. What is the name of the mythical maverick steer that makes an appearance during the celebration in Rodanthe called Old Christmas?

A. Ol' Buck.

15
Unusual Grave and Burial Stories

They Really Danced on His Grave

In the town of Wilson is a lovely burial ground called Maplewood Cemetery. The stones and funerary art alone are worth a visit, and local historian Lu-Ann Monson supplied this tidbit behind one of its more intriguing graves.

Near the front of the cemetery you'll find a tombstone marking the remains of the high diver, Professor Antoine Danton. His act included leaping from a high tower into a small container of water on the ground below.

When he and his circus troupe came to Wilson to perform, he fell in love with a young girl. His traveling lifestyle apparently did not suit her stay-at-home tastes, so his love was unrequited.

He grieved for his lost-love-that-never-was, and one night before performing in Goldsboro, he became inebriated. It was in this state of intoxication that he took his final and fatal dive. According to one historian, Danton was aiming for his target of a flaming hoop that marked the pool of water below, but the wind blew out the fire and he missed.

Conscious but mortally wounded, Danton asked his circus friends to see that he was buried in Wilson, his beloved's hometown, in Maplewood Cemetery. His fellow performers not only honored his request, but on their occasional return trips to Wilson, visited his grave, where they danced and performed at his burial site.

His tombstone reads:

> *Professor A. Danton*
> *Died May 13, 1904*
> *The intrepid high diver leaped from life into eternity at Goldsboro, NC, the night of May 13, 1904. Erected by the J.J. Jones Carnival Co. of which organization deceased was, at the time of his fatal leap, a member.*

Did You Know? Raleigh's Oakwood Cemetery, adjacent to the Victorian-era neighborhood of Historic Oakwood, contains more than forty thousand graves, including twenty-eight hundred Confederate soldiers, several U.S. senators, five Civil War generals, and seven governors.

The Old Burying Ground in Beaufort

In the lovely coastal town of Beaufort lies an ancient cemetery. It holds the remains of many people, some with unusual tales behind their interment. One grave contains the body of a young girl, buried in a rather unusual "coffin."

Shirley Pleace and Carolina Willis, docents with the Beaufort Historical Sites, also lead tours of the Old Burying Ground and volunteered this tale.

In the 1700s, a family from England with the last name of Sloo settled in Beaufort with their infant daughter. When she was a little older, she asked to go visit relatives across the ocean. The father was agreeable and wanted to take his little girl to visit the family in England, but her mother would have none of that—she feared for her daughter's safe return.

After some persuasion, however, the mother relented. She made the father promise that he would return their daughter to her in Beaufort.

The mother's intuition turned out to be correct, and the little girl died on the return voyage from London. Through his grief, the father remembered his promise that he would return their daughter to Beaufort.

To do that, her body would have to be preserved. The father purchased a keg of rum from the captain and immersed his daughter's body in it to preserve her. This was how she returned home to her mother. The little girl's body, in fact, was buried in the keg of rum. Her grave is marked by a flat stone slab, a wooden marker, and a juniper tree.

Now the tale is related to everyone who takes the Old Burying Ground tour. School children often leave small items such as shells and pennies on the young girl's grave.

Another Old Burying Ground story tells of an unknown but loyal British officer who fell grievously ill while stationed on his ship at anchor in the port of Beaufort. Before he died, he requested he be buried in full uniform, standing up, and facing England, with his right arm up in a final salute to King George. His inscription reads:

> *Resting 'neath a foreign ground,*
> *Here stands a sailor of Man George's crown*
> *Name unknown, and all alone,*
> *Standing the Rebel's Ground.*

The Culture of Death in the South

Southerners in general respond to deaths in a way that sets the region apart. When someone passes away in the South, everyone gets to cooking, especially in traditional Tarheel homes. You don't arrive empty-handed at a wake. You are expected to come with a covered dish, preferably something you made yourself (no fast-food fried chicken, no sir). If the body is on view at a funeral home, then the table is set up at the home of the nearest relative, to be laden with everything from chicken and dumplings to barbecue and coleslaw, corn bread, and always lots of desserts. Most often, the foods brought are dishes that the deceased would have enjoyed—a quaint way to pay respects to the dead.

James and Martha Pearl Villas are a famous mother-and-son team from an "old family" hailing from Charlotte. They have produced a number of cookbooks reflecting the flavors of the South, most notably *My Mother's Southern Desserts* (New York: William Morrow & Co., 1998). James is the editor of *Town & Country* magazine, and although he now lives in New York State and cooks with "Yankee flour" (flour made from wheat grown in Yankee country), he's still a Tarheel at heart.

The following recipes are what Martha Pearl Villas refers to as "bereavement dishes." Try them for your next "bereavement" and see what a comfort they can bring.

Bereavement Chocolate Bread Pudding

2 cups finely grated stale white bread

2 cups milk, scalded (see note below)

⅔ cup granulated sugar

2 ounces unsweetened baking chocolate, melted

1 teaspoon pure vanilla extract

½ cup chopped pecans or walnuts

1 cup heavy cream, whipped to stiff peaks

In a large mixing bowl, combine the grated bread and scalded milk and let stand for 15 minutes. Preheat the oven to 350 degrees. Grease a 1-quart baking dish.

Add the sugar, chocolate, vanilla, and nuts to the bread mixture and stir until well blended. Scrape the mixture into the prepared baking dish and bake until a cake tester or straw inserted in the center comes out clean, about 1 hour. Serve the pudding hot in dessert bowls with the whipped cream on top. Makes 6 servings.

Note: When scalding milk in a saucepan, stir continuously over moderate heat to prevent a film from forming. Never allow the milk to come to a boil, and remove the pan from the heat the moment steam begins to rise.

Funeral Angel Bavarian

2 envelopes unflavored gelatin

½ cup cold water

2 cups milk

4 large eggs, separated

1 cup granulated sugar

2 tablespoons all-purpose flour

¼ teaspoon salt

Grated rind of 1 large orange

¼ cup fresh orange juice

1 pint heavy cream

1 10-inch angel food cake

Grated coconut from 1 small coconut

In a small bowl, sprinkle the gelatin over the water to soften, and set aside.

In a large, heavy saucepan, whisk the milk, egg yolks, sugar, flour, and salt until well blended. Cook over moderate heat, stirring constantly, until the mixture thickens. Remove from the heat, whisk in the gelatin mixture, and let cool completely, stirring several times. Add the orange rind and orange juice and stir until well blended.

In a medium-sized bowl, beat half the cream with an electric mixer until stiff peaks form, and fold into the cooled custard. Wash and dry the beaters. In a large mixing bowl, beat the egg whites until stiff but not dry peaks form, and gently fold them into the custard.

Break the angel food cake into small pieces and line the bottom of a large tube pan with half the pieces. Cover with half of the custard, then repeat the procedure with the remaining cake and custard, ending with custard. Cover with plastic wrap and let stand overnight in the refrigerator.

Turn the cake out onto a cake plate. In a medium-sized mixing bowl, beat the remaining cup of cream with an electric mixer until stiff peaks form and spread over the top of the cake. Sprinkle the coconut all over the top. Makes 12 to 14 servings.

When Is a Headstone a Footstone?

Just north of Charlotte in the pleasant town of Salisbury, a train running the railroad line of the Richmond and Danville Railroad on one November night in 1893 caught a man unaware (or others say inebriated) and ran over him—at least, part of him.

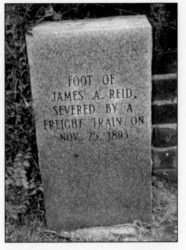

The train left James Reid with a severed foot. Although Reid eventually recovered, he wanted to do something special for his foot. So he buried his foot with what the *Salisbury Post* described as "appropriate ceremony," and a proper headstone was erected with this inscription:

The headstone (or would you call it the footstone?) of James Reid can be seen in the cemetery of Trading Ford Baptist Church. (COURTESY SHEELAGH DONALDSON)

Foot of
James A. Reid
Severed By a
Freight Train on
November 25, 1893

When Reid died in 1920 at age ninety-five, he was buried in the cemetery of Trading Ford Baptist Church, six miles away from his "other" headstone.

Today, many people come to visit these two old graveyards on account of what James Reid did with his bodily parts.

Did You Know? Some lesser-known folks, related to more well-known folks, who lie at rest in the Tarheel State include

★ **Squire (George) and Sarah Boone:** Daniel Boone's parents, buried in Joppa Cemetery, near Mocksville, Davie County

★ **Annie Carter Lee:** General Robert E. Lee's daughter, buried in Jones Springs, Warren County

★ **Marshal Michael Ney:** Napoleon's famous general, believed to be buried under the alias of schoolteacher Peter Stewart Ney in Cleveland, Rowan County

★ **Martha Douglas:** wife of Stephen A. Douglas, buried in Reidsville

The Bodies above the Tunnel

To build the Dillsboro-Murphy rail line, the Danville Railroad Company (which succeeded the Western North Carolina and Norfolk Southern Railroad companies) had to cut a tunnel through a mountain of nearly solid granite along a bend in the Tuckasegee River near Dillsboro. As was customary in those days, the railroad used prison inmates for this arduous task. Every workday, the convicts were ferried across the Tuckasegee River to the tunnel site, where they labored with pickaxes, cutting and chipping away at the mountain.

Eventually the convicts finished carving out the 186-foot passageway, known now as the Cowee Tunnel. Unfortunately, not all of the prisoners survived the tunnel construction project. The story goes that several of the convicts were on the ferry, crossing a particularly treacherous stretch of the Tuckasegee. The ferry was a flatboat, moved across the river by cables. The convicts were shackled together, and when their boat capsized, all nineteen of the poor fellows drowned in the raging waters of the Tuckasegee. Their bodies were recovered and buried on top of the tunnel.

Today this line is used for the Great Smoky Mountains Railroad, and passengers are temporarily plunged into near-total darkness in a section of the tunnel with a sixteen-degree curve. Some people say you can hear the screams of the convicts and even see them, as you ride in the dark tunnel, directly underneath their burial site.

N★C Strange . . . but true

In Hatteras Village is a macabre leftover from the turn-of-the-century sailing days. Here four barrels of human bones are buried. When villagers found decomposed sailors' remains on their beach, they put them in salt-pork barrels and buried them. The "barrel of bones" cemetery is unmarked and undisturbed, to discourage vandalism.

Wilmington's Oakdale Cemetery

If ever you visit Wilmington, be sure to take an afternoon tour of the Oakdale Cemetery. Besides viewing its beautiful funerary art and moss-covered mausoleums, you may learn of tales both tragic and mysterious.

The cemetery was established in the 1800s because the city ran out of room in its local churchyard cemeteries after Wilmington was ravaged by epidemics of yellow fever, diphtheria, and typhoid. A sixty-five-acre site east of Burnt Mill Creek was chosen, and Armand J. de Rosset, a prominent local doctor, became the first president of the board of directors of Oakdale Cemetery. Shortly after this, de Rosset's own six-year-old daughter, Annie, fell ill and died, and was the first interred in the new cemetery. Visitors can see Annie's grave today—it's an upright marker with a little lamb on top of the stone.

Walking around the cemetery, you'll also find a stone with a sculpted image of a dog and the words "Faithful Unto Death." The story goes that in 1880, riverboat captain William A. Ellerbrook was caught under a flaming timber when helping to fight a fire downtown. His dog, Boss, rushed into the flames to try to retrieve his master. Unfortunately, Boss was overcome by smoke and died along with Ellerbrook. Later, the body of the heroic Boss was found with bits of his master's coat in his teeth. Some locals say that Boss still patrols the grounds of Oakdale Cemetery, watching out for his master.

The cemetery is also the final resting place of hundreds of Confederate soldiers in unmarked graves. Some local people say the cemetery is haunted with the wandering spirits of these brave men.

Guess Who? This Cherokee Indian chief's grave is in Graham County. He died in 1814, fighting along with Andrew Jackson against the Creek Indians in the Battle of Horseshoe Bend. His grave is on a hill overlooking the town that bears his name.

Who was this man? Chief Junaluska.

Poetic Immortality

About fifteen miles outside Robbinsville lies a beautiful forest of tulip poplar, hemlock, and cedar trees, with rich dark soil and an abundance of wildflowers and birds. The forest of nearly eighteen thousand acres has trees that tower as high as one hundred feet, many as big around as twenty feet. This forest is a protected area, named in memory of someone who was not a native of the Tarheel State.

Alfred Joyce Kilmer was born in New Jersey in 1886, and after graduating from Columbia University in 1908, worked as an editor for the Funk and Wagnall Dictionary Company. His love of words led him to poetry. By the time America and Germany were embroiled in war, Kilmer was married with five children, and he enlisted in the New York National Guard. Once in France, although his primary job was intelligence gathering, Kilmer wanted to help fight. On July 30, 1918, he died in the Battle of Ourcq.

His name would not be memorable had it not been for his poetry, especially his most famous poem "Trees." Published in 1914, this poem became a part of virtually every student's introduction to poetry, and Kilmer was assured immortality.

In 1935 a forester noted that Graham County held "one of the very few remaining tracts of virgin hardwood in the Appalachians." He recommended that the area be purchased to preserve some of the last remaining original forest growth in the mountain area. When the Veterans of Foreign Wars found out about the setting aside of more than thirteen thousand acres, they asked the American government to make it a memorial to Kilmer. Thus from New Jersey to France to North Carolina, the story comes full circle, and a memorial forest is forever preserved in the name of Joyce Kilmer.

You can hike the trails and footbridges of Joyce Kilmer Memorial Forest, take in its peace, and breathe in the fresh aroma of hemlock trees. Halfway on the trail is a bronze plaque with a brief biography of Kilmer. At the base of the trail under a protected stand is the poem for which Kilmer will be forever remembered.

Visitors to Joyce Kilmer Memorial Forest can enjoy the trees that inspired his famous poem. (COURTESY N.C. DIVISION OF TOURISM, FILM, AND SPORTS DEVELOPMENT)

Trees

I think that I shall never see
A poem lovely as a tree.

A tree whose hungry mouth is prest
Against the earth's sweet flowing breast;

A tree that looks at God all day,
And lifts her leafy arms to pray;

A tree that may in summer wear
A nest of robins in her hair;

Upon whose bosom snow has lain;
Who intimately lives with rain.

Poems are made by fools like me,
But only God can make a tree.

The Mysterious Disappearance of Peter Dromgoole

One of the most pleasant views of the Piedmont area of North Carolina is from the summit of Piney Prospect at the University of North Carolina in Chapel Hill. One of the mysteries of North Carolina is here, a huge boulder with slight reddish hues. The boulder and the red stain unaffected by weather provide the setting for a local legend.

The boulder was once a meeting spot between a young university student, Peter Dromgoole, and his sweetheart, Fanny. It was 1831, so the story goes, and they were desperately in love. Here, sitting on this boulder, Peter and Fanny shared stolen moments with the view of the valley below and the burbling of a spring nearby.

But another young man desired Fanny's affections, and he lost his head with jealousy at the thought of Peter and Fanny together. Finally, the rejected suitor challenged Peter to a duel. Unbeknownst to Fanny, Peter accepted. He and the rejected suitor chose their seconds and met one night at the boulder under a full moon. Peter was killed in the duel, and the witnesses and the rejected lover buried Peter under the boulder, which was stained with his blood.

Fanny returned the next day, and the day after that, and the day after that, hoping to see her love. She wept, sitting or lying prostrate on the boulder under which her Peter lay. Eventually, Fanny died of a broken heart.

There really was a Peter Dromgoole, but no one really knows what became of him. Some say he failed college and entered the military; other people said that they spied him in the streets of Wilmington. At any rate, he never reappeared, and his legend is a part of Chapel Hill.

The boulder that legend says is Peter's burial site is now called Dromgoole Rock, and the spring nearby has been named Fanny's Spring.

Did You Know? In Ocean Isle Beach, Thomas Shannon's casket sales are booming—but not for humans. Shannon owns T&S Pet Memorials, which caters to grieving pet owners. Since starting the business a few years back, Shannon has found his niche in the casket business. Shannon's standard wooden pet coffins start at $60; lace, a pillow, and padded lining can be added for $200. The company makes caskets for birds, pet headstones, and even urns for pet ashes, and offers bouquets with chew toys as added decoration.

A Mysterious Burial Ground

At the Tennessee-North Carolina border town of Bryson City lies a place the Cherokee call Kituhwa (gah-DOO-ah). It is revered by the Cherokee as the birthplace of the People, where the Great Mystery handed down the laws by which they would live. It is also said to be the first earthly home of fire sent by God to his People.

This area has been inhabited for at least nine thousand years. British traders who arrived during the seventeenth century took Cherokee women for their wives and brought European crops to blend with the native ones.

Such activity made Kituhwa the largest and most important village in the valley. In 1720 its population swelled to nearly two hundred. By 1750 Kituhwa contained more than sixty houses, complete with gardens of corn and squash. But a friendly relationship with the British soured as more white men arrived, and in 1761 British troops attacked. With their broadswords, they slashed hundreds of acres of corn and other crops and burned the village to the ground.

On this site in the summer of 2001, archaeologists arrived with scientific equipment, searching for the magnetic "signature" left behind by burned earth. Using gradiometers to measure differences in magnetism in the soil, archaeologists traced a grid-like pattern across the fields of Kituhwa. The scientists were looking for a pattern of burnt earth, like that made by a house burning down.

What they found were the traces of stockade-like walls, the remains of burned houses, and a mound, measuring five feet high and forty-five feet wide. The most dramatic area is in two arcs, which might be from stockade walls or burned houses. Then the researchers found the long mound, the octagonally shaped townhouse that was Kituhwa's center for civil and spiritual fellowship. In its heart had burned the coals from the original Sacred Fire. Near this mound, are as many as a thousand graves inside the old settlement, with more than a dozen outside the settlement itself.

Once under the auspices of the Great Smoky Mountains National Park Service, this birthplace of Cherokee culture has been returned to the descendants of those who lost it during the Trail of Tears nearly two hundred years ago. "The majority of the people want to see this area preserved," says Brian Burgess of the Tribal Historic Preservation Office at the Eastern Band of the Cherokee's Tribal Offices. Burgess himself participated in the dig and the research. "If there is any kind of development, it will be culturally sensitive—something that might accent the integrity of the tradition."

The site is significant because it is the "Mother Town" from which all the belief systems and culture of the Cherokee People originated. Burgess says the site is sacred. "If you lose any type of archaeological resources, the integrity of the site is gone," he adds. "Some of those graves are hundreds, even thousands, of years old."

Intriguing Epitaphs

Here are some tombstone inscriptions from burial sites around the state. These beautiful cemeteries are loaded with history, symbolism, and local lore.

From St. James Churchyard in Wilmington:

> *Slave to no sect,*
> *No private path he trod,*
> *But looked through Nature*
> *Up to Nature's God.*
> —from the grave of Cornelius Harnett

The epitaph on Thomas Wolfe's tombstone in Asheville's Riverside Cemetery is one of the most poignant in the state. (PHOTOGRAPH BY THE AUTHOR)

How loved, how valued once
Avails thee not;
To whom related or by whom begot.
A lump of dust alone remains of thee
It's all thou art and the proud shall be.
—from an unidentified grave

From a small cemetery near Winston and Connor dormitories in Chapel Hill, this tombstone contains words from the UNC fight song:

I was a Tarheel born
I was a Tarheel bred
Here I lie
A Tarheel dead
—from an unidentified grave

From the Honeycutt Family Cemetery in Stanley County:

Whitley, William "Uncle Billy"
December 17, 1775–April 4, 1890.
He cut a full third set of teeth.

In case you were wondering, the dates on Uncle Billy's epitaph are correct. According to newspapers of the time, he lived to be 115 years old, giving him plenty of time to cut all those teeth.

N★C GRAVEYARD TRIVIA

Q. What cemetery contains the remains of Charles F. Fisher (for whom Fort Fisher is named)?
A. The Old Lutheran Cemetery in Salisbury.

Q. What is the only soil in America dedicated as British soil, so English merchant seaman could be buried in their motherland?

A. Ocracoke's British Cemetery, dedicated as British soil during World War II, under the influence of government agent Aycock Brown.

Q. What cemetery contains the mass graves of 11,700 Union soldiers who died as prisoners of war?

A. Salisbury National Cemetery.

Q. What was the nickname of the Italian carnival worker killed in 1911 in Laurinburg, whose real name was Forenzio Concippio and whose body was mummified and displayed for over sixty years at McDougal's Funeral Home until protests caused his body to be buried properly?

A. Spaghetti—because no one could pronounce his real name!

Q. Who is buried in Franklin County inside a large granite boulder covered with a marble slab?

A. William Jeffreys, who was a state senator from 1844 to 1845.

VIRTUAL NORTH CAROLINA

Major Websites with Links

North Carolina (comprehensive site; if you can't find it here, you probably
don't need it): www.internets.com/snorthcarolina.htm (*Note:* the *s*
before North Carolina makes it seem as though it's only concerning
southern North Carolina but it's state-wide.)

North Carolina (general and tourism site): www.visitnc.com

North Carolina (official state site): www.ncgov.com

North Carolina Encyclopedia (on-line version):
www.statelibrary.dcr.state.nc.us/

Major City Websites

Asheville: www.exploreasheville.com

Charlotte: www.charlottecvb.org

Greensboro: www.greensboronc.org

Raleigh: www.raleigh-nc.org OR www.raleighcvb.org

Wilmington: www.ci.wilmington.nc.us/

Winston-Salem: www.visitwinstonsalem.com

Nature, Hunting, Hiking, Fishing, Sports

American Whitewater (general whitewater source):
www.americanwhitewater.org

Corolla Wild Horse Fund: www.corollawildhorses.com

Cycle North Carolina: www.ncsports.org/CycleNorthCarolina

Duke University Sports (Blue Devils): www.goduke.com

Forest History Society: www.foresthistory.org.

GORP (fishing, hiking, paddling, etc.):
    www.gorp.com/gorp/location/nc/nc.htm

Grandfather Mountain: www.grandfather.com

Guide Horse Foundation: www.guidehorse.com

Headwaters Outfitters (western North Carolina paddling, family
    canoeing): www.headwatersoutfitters.com

Insiders' Guide, Fishing, Boating, and Watersports:
    www.insiders.com/crystalcoast/main-fishing.htm

North Carolina Department of Environmental and Natural Resources:
    www.ehnr.state.nc.us/

North Carolina Division of Tourism, Film, and Sports Development:
    www.visitnc.com

North Carolina Fishing and Hunting Link:
    www.members.aol.com/twag2/fish.html

North Carolina Golf Marketing Alliance: www.golf-nc.com

North Carolina Ski Areas Association: www.appskimtn.com

North Carolina Sportsman (comprehensive sports):
    www.northcarolinasportsman.com

North Carolina State University: www.ncsu.edu

North Carolina Wildlife Resources Commission: www.ncwildlife.com

North Carolina Zoo (Asheboro): www.nczoo.org

Paddle North Carolina (whitewater rafting, canoeing, kayaking):
    www.paddlenorthcarolina.org

Sea Turtle Project: www.seaturtlehospital.org

Topsail Island: www.topsoilcoc.com

Transylvania County (Land of Waterfalls): www.visitwaterfalls.com

University of North Carolina: www.northcarolina.edu

Wreck Diving: www.nc-wreckdiving.com

Film, Entertainment, Music

Folkmoot International Festival: www.folkmoot.com

John C. Campbell Folk School: www.folkschool.org

Lexington, North Carolina, World-Famous Barbecue:
    www.visitlexingtonnc.org

Music Maker Relief Foundation: www.musicmaker.org

North Carolina Department of Agriculture and Consumer Services (food,
    fairs, recipes, etc.): www.ncagr.com/index.htm

North Carolina Drama and Theater: www.ncarts.org

North Carolina Film Commission: www.ncfilm.com

TrailerGhosts.com: www.trailerghost.com

The Wilkes Playmakers (Tom "Dooley" Dula play):
    www.wilkesplaymakers.com

History, Art, Museums, Railroads

Battleship North Carolina: www.battleshipnc.com

Biltmore House and Estate: www.biltmore.com

Buddhist Association of North Carolina (the Buddhist temple in Bolivia):
    www.wisecom.com/wat/

Cape Fear Scots/Flora Macdonald Highland Games:
    www.capefearscots.com

Cherokee Reservation: www.cherokee-nc.com

Coastal Guide, Fort Macon: www.crystalcoast.com/fortmacon/

Find a Grave (genealogical and historical research):
    www.find-a-grave.com

Fort Fisher State Historic Site: www.ego.net/us/nc/ilm/tts/ftfisher.htm

International Civil Rights Center and Museum (Greensboro):
    www.sitinmovement.org

Lighthouse stories and photos: www.outer-banks.com AND
    www.bansemer.com/lighthouses

North Carolina Civil War Map of Battles:
www.americancivilwar.com/statepic/nc.html

North Carolina Lighthouses:
www.itpi.dpi.state.nc.us/caroclips/homepage.html

North Carolina Maritime Museum (Beaufort):
www.ah.dcr.state.nc.us/sections/maritime

Queen Anne's Revenge: www.ah.dcr.state.nc.us/qar

Riverside Cemetery, Asheville: www.ci.asheville.nc.us/parks/riverside.asp

Roadsideamerica.com, North Carolina (comprehensive attractions):
www.roadsideamerica.com/map/nc.html

Tweetsie Railroad: www.tweetsie-railroad.com/history.html

INDEX